DYING TO DIET

Help for Those on a Self Destruct Path with Food

•

JUNE BRERETON

Trafford
PUBLISHING

Order this book online at www.trafford.com/07-2816
or email orders@trafford.com

Most Trafford titles are also available at major online book retailers.

Note for Librarians: A cataloguing record for this book is available from Library
and Archives Canada at www.collectionscanada.ca/amicus/index-e.html

Printed in Victoria, BC, Canada.

ISBN: 978-1-4251-6181-1

*We at Trafford believe that it is the responsibility of us all, as both individuals
and corporations, to make choices that are environmentally and socially sound.
You, in turn, are supporting this responsible conduct each time you purchase a
Trafford book, or make use of our publishing services. To find out how you are
helping, please visit www.trafford.com/responsiblepublishing.html*

*Our mission is to efficiently provide the world's finest, most comprehensive
book publishing service, enabling every author to experience success.
To find out how to publish your book, your way, and have it available
worldwide, visit us online at www.trafford.com/10510*

www.trafford.com

North America & international
toll-free: 1 888 232 4444 (USA & Canada)
phone: 250 383 6864 ♦ fax: 250 383 6804
email: info@trafford.com

The United Kingdom & Europe
phone: +44 (0)1865 722 113 ♦ local rate: 0845 230 9601
facsimile: +44 (0)1865 722 868 ♦ email: info.uk@trafford.com

10 9 8 7 6 5 4 3 2

I wish to thank all those who have contributed both with their individual stories and the diary extracts used in the book. All given freely, only the names have been changed to protect their anonymity.

Thank you Brian, my patient and loving husband, you helped me enormously throughout the process of writing and creating both the book and website. I also wish to thank my dear friends for their help and contributions and Judith Charlton who helped so much with its editing and presentation.

You can contact me June Brereton through my web site

www.dyingtodiet.co.uk

I look forward to receiving some excerpts from your diaries to add to my website so that others will benefit from knowing they are not alone in their personal struggle. I hope that by reading my book and answering some of the questions posed for you throughout, you will gain insight into your sometimes tortured relationship with food and improve your relationship with yourselves.

Warm wishes
June

Contents

INTRODUCTION

I have spoken to many people who struggle with a food issue. Some of their stories are both horrifying and fascinating, mainly because I can recognise aspects of myself in all of them. Some describe their craving as an internal emotional and psychological struggle. They talk of gluttony and describe the agonies they endure around what to eat. Many proclaim a love of fatty foods and describe how imagination draws them towards rich, carbohydrate enhanced meals. They talk of an emotional struggle some of which is not to do with here and now but more to do with the negative messages from the past, self criticism, self disgust, anger, sadness and chronic anxiety. You will find some of these stories in the book and I hope that they will help you connect.

Those of us who struggle within the cycle of eating and dieting are aware of the dangers of obesity, yet we continue to eat the wrong kinds of food. We know that obesity can cause heart problems, diabetes, raised cholesterol, circulation and digestive problems and according to the latest research, cancer, just as smoking does. There is a government health warning on cigarettes but does it make much difference to those who really want to smoke? Bad publicity does not deter those who want to use these products, drugs kill and yet those who are addicted continue to use. Does it make any difference to have the information? No, because there is an innate need to self harm. Something drives each person whatever their addiction to do themselves harm. My question is, why? This book explores the reasons and may, I hope give you some insights into what your reasons are for over eating.

In addiction of any kind we seek solace and hope to find it in food, alcohol, drugs and smoking. These cravings take us deeper into a spiralling world of addiction, to a place where emotions and mental torment can be suppressed and denied. By following the addiction one can feel a temporary respite from painful emotions. Satisfying an addiction of any kind puts thinking to sleep, lulls us with a false sense of security, but primarily one has to suffer the push pull of 'shall I or shan't I? Of course we see addiction here at its most difficult, no one uses food to that level, *or do they*?

Only one who is raging a recurrent battle, one who knows what it is like to be fat or addicted knows what all of that feels like. Those who struggle with being over weight or indeed, struggle against it, believe they can eat like other people, sit down to a normal day's intake, and often do so. However each day begins afresh with, maybe, a healthy light breakfast, even a healthy light lunch, as it progresses, the will power we began the day with turns to rebellion and rage. Anger and high levels of anxiety seep slowly into the food addict's blood stream as if a chemical, like Jekyll and Hyde; making the switch within the flick of an eye, fighting the urge to 'let go' to food. A battle fought for a few days eventually is lost and the winner is the food you have eaten.

In all diets there are many suggestions about dealing with cravings for sweet stuff by, for instance, eating an apple or any piece of fruit, even a celery stick, but for the individual who longs for something sweet, a piece of fruit cannot compare with eating chocolate or consuming a whole bag of chocolate brazils. This kind of craving can never be satisfied with fruit, and can only temporarily be fulfilled by chocolate stuffs of any kind. It is an insatiable craving for 'something' and the over eater is rarely able to say what that 'something' is! This is mainly due to the fact that they are only dealing with the superficial aspects of pushing any pain back to where they think it belongs.

For me, looking deep into my unconscious revealed how angry and helpless I have been at various times in my life. Angry with those closest to me, irritated sometimes to a place beyond endurance. Tetchy and angry with them for not knowing me, not listening to my personal struggle, for not noticing me as a child, for the abuse and neglect but of course whatever problems I had with the food issue was not to do with my relationships now. How could I expect my loved ones to understand or make up for what had gone before all those years ago? I cannot relive my childhood and make things better. However, in retrospect I can now see that the anger was eating me up whilst I, in turn, took eating as a way to soothe the internal disharmony. Even more so, I realise that so much of that anger had been masking my fear and anxiety in my daily dealings with life itself. In truth I had carried anger from my childhood. How does a child deal with fear and anger that was never acknowledged?

Overweight people invariably experience physical pains, nausea, headaches, back aches, painful abdominal cramps, emotional yearnings and psychological distress. As a young woman, on my worst days I had to acknowledge that I was a messed up bundle of fibres, mad but not quite certifiable. I remember thinking then how I would like to be in hospital, be a patient in a ward, looked after by others, taken to the toilet, washed and fed with healthy meals, then I would never have to prepare it, control it or make decisions about it. I recognise today that this was about me wanting to be a child again, desiring to rerun the days when, as a child, there was a small chance of some love and care. However the love and care such as it was generally was hazardous.

People who over eat do not long or crave fatty foods, nor do they crave chocolate, or yearn for savouries they only think they do, but they do crave something, and that something can be very elusive. It is linked to so many things some of which we will explore throughout this book.

Whenever a comfort eater is plagued with a craving they invariably go into the kitchen and seek out an answer demanding 'What can I have?' to the kitchen, the fridge, or the Goodie drawer which is more often than not kept for other people who just 'might' want something 'nice' to eat.

In my experience as a therapist there is much in the way of evidence to suggest that all of this is a lack of closeness, care or attention to needs, or something one never managed to attain or sustain as a child. However there is also evidence which points to over indulgence, lack of boundaries and the parent's fear of saying 'No'. 'Over loved' can mean that the parent would find ways to cajole a child into eating rather than allowing him or her to eat what they need. Encouraged to eat everything on the plate is another one. Why? Was it because there were starving children in the world or was it because the parent had a fear of starvation themselves as a child? Post war parenting was based on there not having been 'enough' food due to shortage and rationing, so that the next generation had to be grateful and show appreciation by eating everything put in front of them. A new generation of parents have to face the supermarket each shopping week, buying supplies that are conducive with vast over indulgence.

You, as the reader, may have your own explanation. Was there a shortage of food, love or nurturing or was there an abundance that you did not know how to say no to? I, on the other hand, am not sure if I lacked loved. In a fashion, I was loved but from the position of self-absorption, with parents who sought only to soothe their own distress each tortured in their relationship with the other. They didn't really see me because they were too busy looking at themselves and at each other, fighting out some symbiotic competitive war of who loved whom, or who was in the wrong or right, or who was jealous of whom.

My father was violent and my mother was his victim and yet she stayed with him for fifteen years. Her power was about how she looked and his jealousy proved how much he loved her. Of course, it was all disjointed and dysfunctional but that was about their history and how that history guided their care of me.

After years of dieting, with this fad or that, "Weight-Watchers" and "Slimming World", calorie counting, low fat and "Atkins", the list is endless; for over 30 years of self denial and self deprecation about what a weak woman I was, how stupid I must be to fail so miserably, I can speak with authority on the misguided process of self denial as a form of cure. I see some hope in hypnosis. It offers some cognitive methods of how to change, and however sound, these seem to appear, for the life time dieter, they are still impractical and impossible to maintain. However I am sure the methodology would work if one could find a way to soothe the emotional turmoil that goes along side the desire to lose weight and eat normally so as not to gain weight.

Emotional eating has nothing to do with hunger, only with a deep rooted sense of loss. This kind of loss is not necessarily to do with loss of a person, loved one or way of life. It is to do with the *loss of the self*, low *self esteem* and inability to give oneself love. The majority of fat people are absolutely fantastic in their demonstration of love to those around them. We, in the main are the world's greatest nurturers because we know all the rudiments of what others need. Deep inside we are seeking someone to give it to us. In the paranoid process we are giving to another that which we need, but are unable to recognise or accept for ourselves, even when it is available. While compulsive eating and eating disorders in general might appear to be a preoccupation with food and weight, in the main they are nothing to do with food. Food represents a form of protection. In one way or another, the eating, plays many roles, in the compulsive eater's life. For the CEthere is the sense of lack of control. For the bulimic and anorexic it is about control, controlling what happens to their bodies what goes in and what comes out.

Confused? Of course you are. It is confusing and those with food issues are generally confused. They often make bold untruthful statements about being happy with their body. This is more to do with hiding the shame of being out of control. Being fat is about being ashamed. It has everything to do with shame because being fat is shameful, so often reflected back in the disgust in a slim person's eyes. The shame felt deep inside only manifests through the extra weight. It can also be to do with not seeing a true image of oneself in a mirror. Having a distorted image is familiar to the anorexic but perhaps not so recognisable to the compulsive eater, maybe believing that one is not as fat as one really is.

For a fat person shame is a moment of agonising pain, an implosion hidden behind a laughing face, a jolly personality. There is a need to hide behind the bulk of weight, a massive desire to conceal the terrible sense of low self worth. This must remain unseen at all costs, a process started somewhere way back in childhood.

• Do you recognise any issues of shame or some history of being shamed about yourself, your person, weight, body or sexuality?

Early experiences of food are one of the keys to eating disorders or problems with food in adulthood. As infants we are reliant upon adults to take care of us, nurture, protect and feed us but within so many families there lies a dysfunctional element which is not easily seen.

That dysfunctional element is often about the relationship with the prime carer and how that carer felt about
themselves and you. It is not necessarily to do with how
they fed you, more to do with how they self nurtured,
self cared, what was modelled for you and what their
expectations were of themselves and you. It is also to
do with how well your self esteem was nurtured and
how other members of the family view themselves and
you along with your siblings. My own mother rarely fed
herself by sitting down to a meal; she was always on
one diet or another and eating on the run. As a cook she
would bring home something cooked for 'Her directors'.
Even today at eighty nine years old my mother does not
feel hungry. If you place a good meal before her she
will eat and enjoy it but will rarely cook herself a meal;
quite happy to eat jam and bread and cakes. Cooking
for others and bringing food home for her husband and
children was her one priority as she was ignorant of her
own needs.

Perhaps if you are a part of the commercial world of
slimming, where control and self discipline reign, you
are pulling back from what I am saying because most
want distance from the emotional aspects of weight
gain, and in my experience of slimming clubs, there
is very little space for discussion of how we feel about
being over weight. We are discouraged from looking
back at the whys and encouraged to look forward.
However, I believe that we will never manage to maintain a weight loss until we are allowed to seek out some
links to the past where messages were delivered on a
daily basis. These messages are not always verbal; they
are a way of life that is maintained within the family

and something we will explore later in the book. They are to do with the unspoken and unmet needs of the parent who had their own life issues to contend with. To deal with the past we must link the present together with it.

Beverly had been an only child and her parents had been quite affectionate towards her until her grandmother came to live with them. Beverly found herself pushed into a smaller bedroom and her mother had less and less time for her. Whenever she felt upset or came home from school with problems her parents seemed disinterested and began to give her cake or biscuits to fill the space of their attention. Over the years this pattern continued until one day a 'true friend' pointed out that whenever she seemed upset Beverly would turn to chocolate or cake to deal with her feelings. Over time she came to realise that the past was impinging upon the present and began to look at what she could do instead. She realised that talking to her friend or someone else close to her made a difference. Beverly had never learned as a child how to soothe her own upsets or feelings without food and once she became aware of this pattern she had a choice of changing it. The secret is to become more self aware and then take charge of your own behaviour.

How many of you are able to rhyme off the verbal messages that were passed on, yet not many could highlight, without being counselled, what the psychological messages were. How your parents dealt with food or self esteem issues might be something you have to struggle to remember. One way or another you have listened to the messages from childhood. They are mental implants about meal times, eating and over eating. Phrases like 'eyes bigger than belly' call to mind. 'Greedy guts' and 'who's eaten all the pies' are easy to remember. However parental modelling is more subtle. Of course there may be more damage that will have influenced the way you see yourself in the world; maybe sexual and physical abuse, verbal abuse, hurled insults and subtle jibes from important parental figures. When a child is lonely and unhappy due to the family set up, or where expectations are too high, perhaps no one cared enough to have any expectations at all? How each of us sees our self through the parent's eyes will have influenced self esteem, will power and self worth. It may be true that you had a very happy childhood. That is quite possible but you might want to contemplate how your family dealt with unhappiness, stress and disharmony?

Did they show you how to deal with things that were difficult in life, anger, sadness, fear and so on, or did you all live in a world where everyone was 'happy'?

A mother's image of herself and her own method of self care around food and body will reflect onto her child. It is particularly common in woman to take on the same eating patterns laid down by their mothers. For example mum gets a smaller portion than other members of the family, eats something different. I remember my mother ate '*Limits*' those slimming biscuits that were all the rage in the sixties and seventies, yet she made huge meals for everyone else. She took slimming tablets bought over the counter, which later turned out to be what were known as *'purple hearts'*. She would boast of how she hadn't eaten all day, as if that was right. Worse still, as her daughter I was expected to do the same. Her fear of my gaining weight was horrendous; her image of herself as she compared me to her was terrifying. 'Your bum's too big, your legs are too long; your ankles are thick, look at the size of you'. There was a sense of being shamed and at the same time disowned, with the physical criticisms being so acute a seed of not belonging was planted. I grew up with this distorted image of myself as huge, never realising that none of it was true, instead I became anorexic and later bulimic and as I grew older, turned into my own worst nightmare.

Fat!

As a young girl and woman I repeatedly went through a process of dieting or purging even though I had no excessive weight. In fact, in retrospect I was slim and of normally healthy proportions for my age.

The media today have a lot to answer for. They portray both woman and men as slim and immaculate in everything they do, linking slimness with success and health. However what we see on the media is not to do with health but more to do with need. Many today who work in the media either in fact or fiction are expected to be slim, attractive and clever. Newsreaders, weathergirls, daytime television presenters, ninety-nine percent are slim with a perfect image to be coveted. In drama, mainly American drama, the females are presented to us as thin, not merely slim but a skinny size 0, which is perceived to be glamorous. We do not see many people eating on TV, 'Sex in the City' for example, often showed the main characters as eating in restaurants but they would pick at salad leaves and rarely raise any of it to their mouths, they did however drink alcohol frequently and get drunk. The principal actresses in 'Ali McBeal', 'Desperate Housewives' and 'Friends' over the years of their success became thinner and thinner. Their size, much debated in the media nevertheless became coveted by viewers.

They were the models for the young viewer to see that success and happiness comes with being very slim. This is underscored by the fact that while the papers were on the one hand castigating them for being thin the advertising agencies and fashion industry were snapping them up as models. If one was overweight in these dramas one's life was usually a mess, one was seen as perhaps unlovable or a comic character. Think of how many characters on television you have seen who have been over a size 10. Whenever there is an overweight character they are usually cast as weak or foolish and decidedly plain.

I am not advocating obesity as a good thing; I am merely drawing your attention to the pressure on the viewer which, for those with already low self esteem are given images to which they may never be able to aspire. We are shown advertising copy with close ups of twenty something woman demonstrating how well wrinkle cream works, tall beautiful woman, recommending creams and oils that will be a magic solution to any low self esteem issues to do with the body. Most of whom are presented as airbrushed if not actual 'perfection'.

These days there is enough in the media to publicly shame anyone who is over weight. School children are paraded on the local news described as 'obese', setting them up for public ridicule amongst their peers. Then we have the skinny models, stick insects, parading or should I say 'paraded' in the media. Obviously for them it pays to be anorexic and as such glorified in it. Sadly I think perhaps the Americans do seem to do what they consider to be PC by adding to some soap or other, a fat girl who in the main is generally excellent at doing her job, but not so good in relationships or in bed. It is nonsense of course; being overweight need not make a difference to the way we perform in bed, or the way we feel sexually. I suppose it might inhibit certain positions but in the main being over weight need not affect sexual prowess. We also have programmes about dieting where public shaming about body shape and size are the norm, programmes where small slim woman humiliate obese individuals about how they dress citing weight and appearance as reasons why their partners no longer find them attractive. People who are vulnerable allow themselves to be publicly rebuked so that the viewer can cringe and thank God it isn't them.

I think it important to say that within this book I am not offering some magical answer to losing weight, I am however, offering you an opportunity to look within yourself for the answer as to why you are having a daily battle with food, a struggle to control your own eating habits on a regular basis and a system of yo-yo dieting which is agonising in its very process. I am inviting you to connect the past with the present, to examine and think about whatever has influenced you from your history, and what in that history has impacted upon you to such a degree that you use food as a substitute for love, for self soothing and for suppressing your feelings such as anger, sadness, fear and happiness. I suggest that you use this book like a diary to make notes as you progress and recognise the changes you need to make in your self care. Throughout you will notice I use the terms compulsive eater, over eater or comfort eater. This is because I want you to identify yourself throughout the process of reading the book and you can use which ever you believe applies to you.

CHAPTER ONE

•

WHERE DOES IT START?

'In the cases on which I build my work there has been what I call a true self hidden, protected by a false self. This false self is no doubt an aspect of the true self. It hides and protects it' 'However this hidden true self suffers an impoverishment that derives from lack of experience'.

(D.W. WINNICOTT
CLINICAL VARIETIES OF TRANSFERENCE 1955/56)

Aspects within the family relationships will influence how a child will adapt to suit in order to preserve some sense of security when things become confusing. However in so doing the adaptation becomes what is sometimes known as the false self, protecting the child within from any further abuse. This inner child then remains hidden behind the adaptations. These over adaptations become a way of staying safe and close to others because when we are children we need to stay connected to adults for the sake of survival. As we grow and find the ability to survive alone and where there has been abuse or neglect, we may have lost sight of the real self which has remained hidden and very young. It remains as an immature part of us that has failed to develop.

When we talk of the self we understand this to be the personality and the character. Winnicott, a psychoanalyst (1986) described the way the environment has formed us. But asked, 'Can we really say that the self is as tangible as this?' He stated that each person has a personal and private self that is not available except in intimacy. He was referring to how we present ourselves often in a way that is expected rather than is 'real'.

When a child is sexually or physically abused they might build a defence to protect the self, the child that has been hurt or betrayed by those in his/her environment. This 'real' self becomes hidden emotionally and psychologically, protected from any future hurt. Thus a defensive self will be presented to the world. This could be an over adapted self, or a rebellious self, an angry or depressed self which stands like a suit of armour protecting the real and vulnerable self within. All of this in order to prevent further humiliation, shame, aggression and abandonment. We have all heard of the individual who self harms, cuts themselves to release the distress that has been internalised because of the early abuse or dysfunctional processes in their history. Here the individual is attempting to keep hidden the real self in order to prevent the pain of the past emerging. Many will find a variety of ways of keeping this self suppressed, keeping the lid well and truly fastened down. Food is one way, gaining weight another constantly fluctuating in weight in order to fill one's life with dieting and focusing on food, or maybe doing over obsessive gym activity etc. All are ways of detracting from the pain within.

At birth a child does not have the capacity or ability to self protect or take care of itself. It has to attach in order to survive. As the infant develops it becomes more and more independent. It is important to stress that as parents ourselves we have to remember that we can only be a good-enough-parent, there is no such thing as a perfect parent and we will make mistakes as we go. Being merely good-enough will not harm your child but being careless, abusive, engulfing and cruel will.

As infants we make intuitive decisions about what happens around us. If we are responded to lovingly, and healthily we will learn we are safe and secure. If however we are responded to angrily or left for long periods this will impact upon how we view the world in the future. We may decide that it is safer or easier not to ask for what we want. A double edged sword ensues. Shall we ask or shall we not? Can we? Can't we? Do we or don't we take the risk of abandonment?

As parents we transmit messages to our children both verbally and non-verbally. Non-verbal will be about body language, facial expression, a raised eyebrow the turn of a head, stiffening shoulders and so on. A child will interpret this and make intuitive decisions about self, other and the world around them.

In the book I have mentioned the psychological hungers (Hungers of a Different Kind Chapter 4) I suggest you look at where your needs are when reading this chapter.

In good-enough relationships with a parent a child learns how to self soothe. (Symbiosis chapter 6) If not responded to healthily and reasonably a child experiences over whelming anxiety and they do not have the ability to deal with experiencing a high level of anguish. When this happens a child closes down and dissociates shielding themselves from further distress. A consequence of this is the development of terrible shame or guilt about having needs or feelings at all.

Low self esteem and poor self image and self hate can also ensue, thus it is important to deal with these aspects of the self in order to begin the process of self love.

The acknowledgment of such issues is the beginning of self recognition and good self worth.

In many cases I recommend some counselling or therapy to reach the part of you that has gone underground as a child.

Your Personal Diary Entry

Write down some of your personal responses to what you have just read.
How have you felt whilst reading?
Remember feelings are your emotions, anger, sadness, fear or happiness. What, if anything, rang a bell for you?

_____

_____

_____

_____

_____

_____

_____

_____

_____

_____

_____

_____

_____

Early Years.

With the care it receives from the mother each infant is able to have a personal existence, and so begins to build up what might be called a continuity of being. On the basis of this the inherited potential gradually develops into an individual infant. If however maternal care is not good-enough then the infant does not really come into existence since there is not continuity of being; instead the personality becomes built on the basis of reactions to the environment impingement.

(D.W. WINNICOTT
THE THEORY OF THE PARENT, INFANT RELATIONSHIP 1960)

Although some of you might want to discount family history, familial tendencies, and influences from the past, it is necessary to look back into your personal histories because research reveals that the past has a major part to play in how we look at ourselves, how we learn to deal with our emotions and the events that have been difficult in life.

For many, being overweight can be worn like some form of protective clothing, a defence against aspects of life in childhood that have to be kept buried. Sometimes being big, will act as shield for a small child hiding in a large body where no one can harm or touch them. It is often a way keeping hidden from society ones own internal sense of shame, despair and terror, using food as a form of shelter, from both the outside world and the internal conflict. Of course this only leads to more shame, lower self esteem and so on; a cycle of despondency, despair, and anguish, which seems impossible to escape from. When a person has low self esteem and poor self worth it will influence all aspects of life.

Compulsive eating involves a complex collection of behaviours, hiding the emotional pain by presenting a different self to the world than the real self. The compulsive eater is constantly tested by those around them and by the expectations of others. Most compulsive eaters have a heightened awareness of other people. Many hold a paranoid view of the world, watching others watching them so to speak. Invariably they experience a sense of being observed by those in their immediate environment, but this is something noticed just beneath conscious awareness. An individual with low self esteem often views the world through another person's eyes. If I suggested to an obese person they may be paranoid they are likely to jump into denial. However if I suggest that they have low self esteem they would agree whole heartedly. It is a myth to think that those who are overweight do not care how they look. Many who do not have this problem only see what is there, and maybe never consider the suffering that can go on beneath the surface.

- How many over eaters feel self conscious when eating, or buying food in a restaurant?

- How many of you would try to eat sensibly in the public arena?

Why? Because you are aware of other people around you, to such a high level you can find little peace in the public domain.

Numerous over weight people cope with this level of awareness of others by rebellion, perhaps really and metaphorically putting two fingers up to the world. But still there is the self doubt, the longing to be free of another's spoken or unspoken opinion. This opinion may only be imagined but will be based upon the cruel reality of the public view, encouraged by media and magazine articles.

An obese person doesn't need to be told they are overweight, doesn't need to be told that they should lose weight; they already know what society thinks.

Over weight people will invariably choose the lowest calorie foods when eating in public, or take on a nonchalant approach used as a defence against what they perceive society thinks about the way they eat and what is being eaten. Dealing with this requires huge amounts of psychic energy.

In my experience, comfort eating is about having to be attuned to the needs of others in order to deal with what went on in childhood. Generally as a child their own reality has been denied, questioned or ignored. They have spent much of their childhood learning how to be wary of others.

A child who has been sexually abused or treated badly in some way is told by the abuser that what is happening is not real, or that no one will believe them or that they are loved by their abuser. They are so often instructed not to be silly when they become upset or frustrated by what family members are doing and saying.

In the main children who grow up to be over eat ers or compulsive eaters have had their reality denied in some way. In my view this needs to be grieved for. The loss of the self and the significance of self and self care were denied and thus grieving time discounted or acknowledgment of emotional pain, over looked. Emotions will be buried and suppressed, all of which will lie beneath the surface like a wound that never healed, something that food and the internalised struggle with eating will only temporarily soothe, like an Elastoplast on a large festering ulcer.

Even the simplest things that are said to a child can be about denying reality and on a regular basis, over time can lead to self doubt and a sense of inadequacy which may be rebelled against or permanently damage self esteem. Of course there are many levels of low self esteem and even the most extraverted person can have low self esteem or lack confidence in certain aspects of their life. Many of us are good at wearing a front or a mask to hide the pain within. Many have learned to smile and over adapt so that others will not know what is going on.

Why do it?

When we over eat we are generally preoccupied with food, eating and weight. Often this process is about attempting to hide other issues. A compulsive eater uses food to deal with stress, anger, emotional upset and other problems. Food is a temporary measure to suppress some aspects of life. It is often about staying away from overly close relationships whilst carrying a deep rooted fear of abandonment. When we allow others in to our world we exchange loving energy. It gives us a new lease of life. Even short term love and minimal contact, moment to moment intimate interactions with others brings a new sense of pleasure and sense of recognition. In staying with the imagined disadvantages of close contact we stay locked in a secret world where we are alone. It is an early decision, which implies that because giving and receiving love is so painful one is better not to have any at all, better not to give anything of oneself. It is better to have none than feel the pain of the loss when it's gone; therefore one will not allow oneself even the tiniest bit of closeness.

Here the individual is locked in a constant state of self-denial.

- Perhaps in your life you have felt love for something or someone and had it snatched away from you in some way?

- Perhaps as a child the pain of the loss was so great you decided that you would never get that close again?

- Have you built defenses to protect you from the fear of the loss of love?

- If as a child you did not experience enough or any of your parents' love, then you may have decided that you can live without it and therefore, stay in self- protection.

- Maybe as a child you were controlled and over protected, you had to hide your sense of self in order
to exist within yourself.

*When Molly was a little girl her father became ill,
although he stayed at home for a while no one ever dis-
cussed with her what was happening to him. She was
very close to him and loved him very much. A general
consensus within the family was that he was OK. She
could see that he was ill and yet her reality was repeatedly denied even by her father himself. Eventually
he went into hospital and still no one explained that
he was not going to come out. When he died she had
not been taken to the hospital to see him. Of course
he didn't return and eventually her mother told her
quickly that he was dead. It was never spoken of again.
For years Molly believed that everyone was angry with
her and she herself continued to believe, for a long time,
that his death had been something to do with her. Of
course, what we see is that the family could not cope
with the experience of grief, the belief being that its
best left unsaid. It affected her because she had lost her
father and she was never able to experience her feelings
about that. She also made some decision that her feelings were too much for others to handle, so it would be
best to keep them to herself in future.*

Early damage

Attachment is a reciprocal system of behaviours between an infant and a caregiver—generally the mother. The term reciprocal is apt because not only does attachment affect the child's behaviour (for example, moving closer to the mother when stressed), but also affects the responses of the mother, who emits care-giving responses in the presence of signals from the infant.

(JOHN BOWLBY (1982).
ATTACHMENT AND LOSS. VOL. 1: ATTACHMENT 2ND ED.).

We are damaged, to a greater or lesser degree if we use food to soothe, merely continuing something which began in childhood. As a child, mealtimes for me were erratic and very much dependant upon my mother's return home from work. She brought food home in a shopping bag, saved from meals she'd cooked in the day. I used to be so hungry that I would wait for her at the corner of the street so that I could help her carry her bags back to the house. I would feel much better once we went in doors where she would begin to heat up the meal for the family. In retrospect my mother didn't feel hungry because she worked with food, rarely considering how hungry we children were. Today I associate meal times with contact and love and expressions of care. Food meant contact and the warmth of companionship. It meant eating with my loved ones. Entertaining was always about providing food for my guests. At one time if they ever requested something I didn't have in my cupboards or fridge, I would have been mortified.

As children we may be either nurtured by the environment we live in or damaged to a greater or lesser degree, of course there is a wide area between these polar opposites and we could represent that on a scale of 1–10.

1——2——3——4——5——6——7——8——9——10

Where on that scale would you considered yourself nurtured by your environment or damaged by it? **1** is highly damaged **10** is well nurtured. Remember there is good and bad in everything; just get some idea of where you might be in this grey area.

It is important to remember whilst reading the following that some of us have experienced the intensity of terrible abuse perhaps both physical and emotional, whilst others may only have a hint of it. However, we will still have built our defence systems to self protect and to grow into the adults we are today and all abuse is relative to the situation you lived in at the time.

Research has shown that when one or both parents is persistently unresponsive to the child's care and where the parent is actively reproachful and rebuffing of the child on a regular basis, it can lead into them having an expectation that others will reject them. More than likely the individual may set themselves up in life to get what they expect.

It would follow that when an individual had repeatedly modelled for her, (for the sake of ease I will use either gender) rejecting and ignoring attitudes, they are likely to do the same to themselves and to others as they grow older.

> As a child George was ignored by his father. It was as if he wasn't living in the same house. That was, until his father was angry with George's mother. He would then start to put George down saying things scathingly to his wife about their son.
>
> "How could you give birth to such a stupid kid?" Or "He's not my kid who did you sleep with to get him" and so on. George was the verbal punch bag for his father to use in order to persecute his wife. While she on the other hand did nothing to protect her son from these abusive behaviours. Later she would comfort him by feeding him chocolate or cake when what he needed was to be protected and fought for. If she ever tried to stand up to her husband it only served to cause both his parents to row more over his head, using him as the butt of their anger. This fed into George's belief system, seeing himself as unimportant and nonexistent in the eyes of the significant adults in his life. Indeed, existing as a nuisance or irritant to others.

We can recognise how important food became to George throughout his life. To give up comfort eating would mean he had to give up the only form of support and love he had known and learned from his mother. Whilst he continued in this pattern of behaviour he did not grieve for the parents he should have had. To change his eating patterns and lose weight he would need to own the fact that his parents were wrong and what they did was bad. He needed to learn to like and love himself, and see his own needs as important. So he had to give up some misguided belief about his parents care.

We also recognise that where there are disruptions and interruptions to parenting and where the relationship with the parents is disorganised, quite frequently, there will be damage to the sense of self because of the lack of familiarity. This can also include periods in hospital or institutions, boarding schools etc. Of course in modern day hospitals the parents can stay close by, but in the fifties and early sixties, hospitalisation meant that parents were not allowed to visit children in the same way they do today. Where there is an inconsistent pattern of parenting, say if sometimes the parent is around and sometimes not, and where there has been a lack of continuity causing the individual to become highly anxious and expectant of more inconsistency, they may repeatedly steel themselves for rejection or abandonment. Perhaps failing to allow themselves to become attached in case the other does not stay around. Some may even see it as quite acceptable to be rejected or treated badly. A child may come to believe that they are not worth loving, not worth caring about and may react in a number of ways, by rebelling, or running away, being angry and aggressive or they may become extremely anxious in their need to please finding other ways to soothe these feelings that can shift from one extreme to the other. Eating is a way of pushing down feelings. Food can become the one thing that the child can rely upon and to some greater or lesser degree, control. Sometimes a parent may behave in a push, pull way, being affectionate one day and elusive the next, sometimes moody and disparaging, or just not there on a regular basis. An example of this is when a parent makes promises to meet the child outside school to take them out but then not be there, or if they are, change the ground rules to something else. This can be very disturbing to a child if repeated on a regular basis. When parents are separated the father/mother may make promises to visit or take a child out for the day, then just fail to turn up.

> *Jane's mother was an alcoholic, throughout most of the day she was affectionate and loving but could also suffer from bouts of depression. As the day progressed, when Jane came home from school, her mother would promise to make an evening meal. She would be laughing and fun loving with the children, and Jane would be swept along, enjoying the warmth of the kitchen but as her mother began to cook, gradually, things would deteriorate and she would begin to feel anxious when a bottle of wine was opened, The process of cooking and drinking the wine meant a slow deterioration in the meal being completed, let alone eatable. Time would pass and the meal would become more and more elusive and rarely came to fruition. Eventually Jane would end up finding something to eat for her younger sister and herself. This ultimately led Jane to eat erratically and unhealthily. Food became a source of comfort but also a source of frustration.*

John Bowlby's attachment theory revealed that when various phenomena occur in families there are consequences, for example, when the main carer is persistently threatening the child with a withdrawal of love or demonstrates that the child is not loved. This is used as a means of control by parents. An individual may not believe themselves lovable and therefore will discount or dismiss any affection shown or may over adapt in their responses to others in order to stay close. Here we may find the woman who is pleasing to be with, willing to stay late at work or give up something that she wanted for herself in order to do something for someone else. We may have the man who does not see himself as lovable and may seek out employment where he can shine in being structured and ambitious. In these circumstances the individual may be trying unconsciously to prove their worth and may only see themselves as valuable in terms of what they can do or achieve and so on.

> *How can anyone love a naughty girl like you?* Barbara's mother would say regularly, whenever she showed any failure to conform. If Barbara pushed against her mother's boundaries she was told either she didn't love her mother or her mother would withdraw love from her, sulking for long periods of time. Her mother would often shun her, cutting her out by not speaking for several days. Barbara was never sure what she had done to displease, but from this came the urge to please others on a daily basis.

Next we may have a parent who makes threats to abandon a member of the family or child; this is used as a method of discipline or as a way of controlling a spouse therefore observed by the children. An individual may behave in a way that would indicate they would leave you if you let them down. They threaten to leave you before you leave them. As a child Emily's mother was constantly threatening to leave Emily's father, frequently packing her bags just prior to her husband returning from work. Emily and her brother would plead and cry begging their mother not leave them and their daddy. Thus after much begging and pleading by the children, the mother would eventually sit down, cry and the children would try to comfort her, promising to be good and do the chores and so on if only she would stay.

Try to imagine the impact upon a child if you can.

Johnny saw his mother do this repeatedly and experienced a deep rooted fear of being left behind. This prevented him from making lasting relationships with woman. Inside he never expected them to stay and could not guarantee that he would be able to sustain a relationship himself. The one thing he was sure about was where his next meal was coming from because he could control that.

We may have a parent repeatedly making threats to the other partner either to desert or even to kill the other, or to commit suicide. Here the child, once they become grown up, may use the same methods as the parent to find out if they matter, or may not allow themselves to see you as an important figure so that they will never feel the loss of you should you leave or die.

Frank would threaten suicide every time his girlfriend wanted to end the relationship. She wanted to leave him but was frightened by his threats, not wanting to be responsible for the consequences of her actions. In therapy she was able to eventually see that she was not responsible for another grown up and recognise that what Frank was doing was emotional blackmail and not the way to find true love.

When a parent induces a child to feel guilty by claiming that his/her behaviour will be responsible for the parent's health or imminent death, the individual may live in a guilt-ridden system thus taking on any responsibility for things that go wrong in relationships with others. When making adult relationships this individual feels guilty if the partner is ill or depressed or down hearted by something that has nothing to do with them. They want to make everything better but, of course this has its downfalls because they have never learned how to take care of themselves. They place too much emphasis on the happiness of the other and always see themselves as responsible for what is happening to the other.

Clara used to feel very guilty when her husband came home from work feeling tired and complaining of being overworked. She tried very hard to make him feel better and could not tolerate seeing him in a low frame of mind or disappointed about anything. This was because she had never succeeded in making her parents happy, well or contented, so she hadn't felt safe with them and blamed herself for her mother's unhappiness. Clara ate in order to soothe her inner chronic anxiety; food helped her to satisfy the unmet needs from her childhood whilst also making herself feel even more rejectable.

A highly critical parent can induce shame in the child. When a child is brought up in a shame based system they experience excruciating internal suffering and humiliation. Parents say such things as 'You shouldn't have been born; I wish you were dead, you're nothing etc'. In relation to others the individual may continually expect you to shame them and invariably you will. How can you not do so, when the trap is set?

Deep inside there is a sense of being bad or wrong about ones sense of self. Also a parent may make public any negative aspects of the child, causing embarrassment and shame. Here a child may begin to internalise a view of themselves and perhaps hide who they are.

> *Jo's father was very subtle in his criticism of her. He would say things about friends of Jo for example he would compliment one of her friends, 'She's a pretty girl, very well mannered, better than someone I know'.*
>
> *Also, 'Why can't you be more like your cousins, they are always polite and they work hard in school?' His criticism was never direct yet always comparing her to someone else. 'Mary doesn't eat a lot like someone we know'. Jo experienced herself as never measuring up to her father's expectations so eventually she gave up but only to make herself into what he expected her to be. Over weight and failing in many aspects of her life.*

Then there is the over indulgent parent who 'just wants you to be happy'

In this instance the parent allows the child to have or do what they want. Given too many options to choose from, a child cannot make an adult decision and the parent needs to set boundaries and say no without fear of reprisal from their child or children. A parent who cannot set boundaries is still child-like themselves and the children in the family grow up very insecure because they are being parented by a child.

Stanley always maintained he had a very happy child-hood and, of course, he did in many ways; however what was missing was his own ability to set boundaries for himself. He grew up finding it difficult to find the job he liked. He was not able to maintain lasting relationships because he found it difficult to accept responsibility for his actions. He had a child like quality that was lovable but he also had great difficulty in looking after himself because he lacked the discipline to keep fit and lose weight. He found solace in food to soothe some of his internal confusion and distress at not feeling at ease within himself.

- Do you recognise yourself in any or all of the above? Remember you may see aspects of yourself in some of what you read in this book, I encourage you tell your own story in order to draw the connection with how you are today in your process of self nurturing.

- Think back over your own relationship with a parent or parental figures and look into how you adapted to the circumstances.

Child development & attachment theory

Research has shown that sensitive handling parental styles, influence child development. It also shows how the child learns to deal with the variety of attachment processes that are used and modelled to them by family, and this will influence the way they deal with their own internal system in relation to those around them.

When, as children, we are separated from our main caregivers either in a traumatic way or by loss and separation, for example in circumstances such as hospitalisation, loss of a parent, or by a parent threatening to leave, or where there is confusion within the family set up, the child will experience three major stages

1. **Protest** by crying and refusing to be consoled.

2. **Despair** where the child is sad and becomes passive

3. **Detachment** in where the child actively disregards and avoids the parent on their return.

Sensitive responding by parents must influence a child's development—i.e., it must make a difference
(LAMB, THOMPSON, GARDNER, CHARNOV, & ESTES, 1984).

Eating problems, as in the compulsive eating process in all its levels are a defence mechanism, or are indeed a learned method of dealing with the awful over whelming emotions that accompany the unresolved grief experienced as a child.

Most behavioural studies show that children being born into situations that are scanty in care and nurturing will experience a very negative effect which will impact upon the adult personality throughout. How, as children, we perceive the parents' response to us will affect the way we in turn react in relation to others and indeed to ourselves when under stress. We will continue to treat ourselves as we were originally treated in many aspects of self care.

Through out generations one improves upon the other. Each generation will in the main, improve both in education and in social aspects of life in general, however emotional and psychological well being is something that may not change. This will be linked to self esteem and self worth, which can lie hidden beneath a polished exterior, handed down like a hot potato from one generation to the next.

Your Personal Diary entry

Write your personal responses to what you have read so far.
Make a note of what you think and feel, it will help you remember what has been useful to you.

_____

_____

_____

_____

_____

_____

CHAPTER TWO

•

ATTACHMENTS
AND
COMFORT EATING

Driven to Attach

A human's first instinct is to seek emotional contact with another human being. We are driven to attach and this attachment is a source of love, warmth and protection. The infant must seek close proximity to stay safe in the world. It was Freud who described it as Motivation in life. He described *Libido* as the will to live and seek attachment, *Aggression* as the drive to make things happen, and *Morbido*, as the knowledge of the inevitability of death and loss.

Research has shown that the individual who experienced attachment issues has been exposed to disruptions in the attachment process as a child. We develop our ways of being with others through our observations as children. How do the grown ups behave with each other, toward each other and so on? What we observe and personally experience will influence the way we live our lives in the future.

When we talk about attachment what do we mean? There has been much research done on the subject which indicates its significance in our personal development.

As infants we have to make an attachment in order to survive. We seek it out and find safety. As infants, everything about us is attractive. We are tiny. We smell sweet. We are vulnerable, which invites the adult to protect and care for us. Early ruptures in attachments can impair the development of the real self and the individual may be driven into unbearable loneliness, helplessness and depression which become a part of development from then on.

Ainsworth and her colleagues (1971) published studies in child management and development, revealing principal patterns in the formation of attachment and what happened within the family system to promote certain aspects of the personality to emerge. I aim to demonstrate a connection between over eating, comfort eating and your relationship to food in general. I am highlighting characteristics of attachment so that you might recognise aspects of yourself and link it to how you deal with food.

Secure attachment

This implies dependability in the main carer, one that provides a safe and secure environment, in which the child is confident that his/her parents will be available, responsive and helpful should s/he encounter adverse or frightening situations. This reassurance gives a child a feeling of being bold in the exploration of his world.

It means the parent is being readily available and sensitive to a child's signals and lovingly responsive when s/he seeks protection and comfort. Here the child can be easily soothed and reacts with only minimal upsets when separated from their main carer, feeling assured that they will return to collect them.

The studies described someone with an **anxious avoidant** pattern of relating to others, demonstrating a reluctance to attach to others because of the early insecure base they lived in. In other words, here we have an individual who has difficulty forming strong and long term relationships with another person. This type of person could be construed as a compulsive self reliant personality. We might see an individual who finds it difficult to get close to another, because they anticipate rejection and humiliation should they be left again, just as in childhood.

In childhood perhaps the parents, one or the other, may themselves have exhibited behaviours indicating that they did not want closeness or intimacy within relationships; possibly showing themselves as unreliable carers just as their parents had been. This parent, as a child, may have shut themselves off from being close due to their own early environmental influences. Sometimes, however they may have decided they would be able to survive as long as they suppressed their needs, indeed, if they didn't show any needs at all. It may have been the only way that particular child could get by and stay in some kind of tolerable relationship with the parent. By doing this they were able to stave off fears of abandonment, keeping a strong sense of anxiety at bay. Thus, as parents themselves they will manage to suppress emotions but appear to their own children as distant and cold and even cruel and unfeeling.

When the individual experiences anxiety in relationships as an adult, it will invariably be because of the original uncertainty in the primary parental care. As a child, if an individual has been prone to separation anxiety, and shown early indications of being clinging and anxious about exploring the world, it will affect the relationships in adult life. Separation anxiety is not something that only children experience. This pattern in the here and now could be construed as jealousy or neediness and possessiveness, all of which puts intolerable pressure on relationships.

> *Peter came from a large family the middle child of five children. His mother had also been the youngest in a large family being brought up mainly by her older siblings. Prior to his birth his sister of three years, the only girl, had died of pneumonia. His mother quickly became pregnant again with Peter giving little or no time to go through a grief process. He described his mother as cold and elusive only picking him up on rare occasions; she seemed uncomfortable when handling him. He believed that his mother disliked him and although desperate to please her, he also felt very anxious in her company as she would frequently push him away. It became clear to him that his mother had been afraid to attach to him for fear of losing him. Comfort eating became a way of staving of the loneliness he felt on so many occasions.*

Then we have what is known as the **anxious attachment** issue. This applies to someone who experiences a high level of anxiety and indecisiveness whilst also having an urge to cling to anyone who they care about. They live life in a constant state of unease, struggling with a feeling of angst lest they experience the pain of abandonment again. We see this person as presenting as more adaptive, leaning more towards being a compulsive care giver. They cannot help themselves from having an urge to please others, behaving and believing as if they themselves are not important. They may also seem child like and not really grow up for fear of taking responsibility and failing in life. Sometimes there has been a double message when a parent has told them not to be childish and yet pressed them to grow up quickly. This individual might be wary, always trying to anticipate what others want in order to retain some semblance of closeness. Some however, may show ambivalence towards relationships indicating aspects of push pull, causing those close to them some level of confusion, one day complying with the others needs the next careless and unfeeling. This is generally due to not knowing what they want themselves, their own needs lost in the eons of time.

Ainsworth later developed (1978) what was named the **disorganised disorientated** attachment process which showed a more chaotic childhood relationship with parents. In this the individual carries a message that they should not exist. They are not wanted and perhaps should not even be alive. Somewhere the parent may have given a psychological message, an unconscious message that the child is OK to exist but it has to be on the parent's terms. By trying to retain some sense of wellbeing and cope with the internalised struggle and emotional upheavals the individual becomes as confused in relationships as they were confused by the original carers. This individual is often suppressing rage and terror in order to survive. Children who are abused or humiliated on a regular basis will live with the fear of annihilation within the original family. This original anger and terror becomes despair and makes a terrible impact upon the individual who experiences depression and futility in adult life. In this instance the individual may attempt suicide or at the very least have a chronic desire to give up on life.

As a psychotherapist, I am well aware of the anxiety caused by separation and loss; most problems in the adult life can be traced back to early separation anxiety, traumatisation and experiences of abandonment. Described as a main source of anxiety in childhood, *'the threats of losing the attachment figure'*. Bowlby (1960) He said that this manifests as depression, self harming life patterns, relationship difficulties, fear of intimacy, suppression of needs and wants, disassociation issues, hiding feelings, low self worth and low self esteem, lack of confidence in certain areas, fear of failure, fear of rejection, chronic anxiety, suicidal issues and so on. The list is endless and will be associated with eating disorders of any kind.

George a 44 year old male came to therapy because he was having problems within his second marriage. His wife complained that he was cold and unfeeling whenever she needed support, at which time he would withdraw physically by going into his workshop and throwing himself into DIY. She had threatened more recently to leave him and he had made a promise to her that he would change. It emerged over time that when George had been nine years old his mother had died from cancer. Almost immediately after the death, without any forewarning, he was sent to stay with his father's parents at the other side of the country. This meant a change of schools, loss of familiarity and the loss of his maternal grandparents and school friends.

George boasted in therapy of how well he had done as a child and reported himself as fitting well into his new life and how the death of his mother had been lost in time. No one talked of it and he eventually after a spell of enuresis began to enjoy school. He was good at sport and found new friends and recognition through his physical activity. His father visited him intermittently over the years to follow and eventually remarried but George remained with his grandparents until going away to university, returning home only for brief periods. He married at 21 which lasted for 2 years and then met and married his second wife in 1997. His paternal grandmother died a few months after the birth of his first child. He reported in therapy that his wife's major irritation was that she saw him as indifferent to her and his daughter.

I hope as you read this you will be analysing your own position in life considering whether you please people or withdraw from them, whether you withdraw, in order to protect yourself from rejection, or from having to take care of them. Maybe you experience a love hate process within your relationships with others, giving help whilst at the same time resentful of their neediness. Perhaps you are always ending up in situations where you have someone to worry about or need to take care of. Perhaps you are the one to whom people look for help, but when it comes to you getting help there doesn't seem to be anyone there, and from here you feel angry and let down which may be a familiar sensation from the past. Also you probably find it difficult to ask for help or know just what you want help with.

Either way you are not being yourself but presenting the false self, the defensive self to the world. I suggest now that you consider if any or all of the above apply to you.

Look at your own history within the family and link the differing methods of learning to attach to how you are today.

- Is it easy to be close to others?

- Do others have expectations of you which you need to live up to?

- Do you experience yourself as feeling guilty if you don't want to do something, or give something of yourself to others?

Consider how you use food to help you cope with your relationship, your disappointments with others or your fear of getting close to other people.

Consider any of the following and see if you can find a link to where and when you started to use food as a way of coping with stress and distress.

- Development issues which are affected by separation and loss in childhood.

- Family relationships and parental disharmony

- Dysfunctional family lives

- Comfort eating encouraged by parent/parental figures

- Over indulgence, abundance

- Rationing of good things or scarcity

- Parenting styles built on self denial

- Negative methods of self soothing taught by parental figures

- Lack of self care stemming negative parenting

Insecure Attachments

Insecure attachments are caused when a child has experienced a parent leaving or threatening to leave or they go away and do not return or if a parent remains unavailable or unresponsive or unhelpful when called upon by the child. Perhaps a child has been punished for relying upon a parent so they learn to avoid seeking help in the future.

Children learn quickly how to live in these and other situations, they find ways to communicate without causing themselves too much distress, finding ways to live in the world and stay safe. Sometimes this means they may have to redefine aspects of their communication. Unconsciously distorting reality in order to match a preferred view of the world and others, for example a person who believes they have to struggle alone against what might be seen as a cold hard world may distort another's kindness and distrust what they are hearing or seeing, perhaps perceiving that the other is trying to get something by manipulation.

We may also use something in our process with others called discounting which means making something worthless when it isn't. We may remain passive, which means we will over adapt to others, act passively/do nothing, agitate, or make oneself ill which is sometimes known as incapacitation, at its worst a person may become unreasonably angry and physically violent.

It is important to note here that all of the above is a way of protecting oneself, coping with getting hurt, humiliated, shamed and worst of all to a child, abandoned.

Your Personal Diary

Are you recognising anything about yourself so far?
If so write it down so that you can refer back if and when you want to.
Think about your own attachment processes.

_____

_____

_____

_____

_____

_____

_____

_____

_____

_____

_____

_____

_____

CHAPTER THREE

•

GRIEF AND LOSS

Perhaps life is truly meant to be directionless? Maybe each one of us fumbles our way down corridors without end, one merging into the next. Each scrabbling down gravel paths, grasping for foot holds, reaching out blindly for something solid to hold on to but finding only shifting sand.

Each of us has a way of surviving and recovering from life's upheavals. As in life we go through stages or phases of development and change, so we pass through a process of development when we grieve in loss. If this process remains incomplete, it may lead to emotional growth impairment. The grief may be fixated at one level, thus healing of the emotional wound remains incomplete, and forming new attachments thereafter, incomplete. As therapists we work with any number of grief issues not just the loss of a loved one. Grief and loss are a part of life and therefore the grief process can be applied to all aspects of living.

Individually we go through life managing problems, getting through them or batting them to one side. We experience relationship difficulties, lack of confidence in areas of work and society in general. Some of us will have problems in attachment and maintaining long term intimate relationships. Many will experience confidence issues, like low self esteem, lack of self worth, and so on.

Remember the importance of acknowledging the historical elements that have helped form your personality.

So far we have been looking at the importance of child development and family analysis such as, how did we become the way we are? What happened within our family history which has helped form the way we see others, ourselves and the world around us? This will influence all aspects of us today. Regularly we meet grief stemming from early on in our development. Unresolved loss issues, which may encroach upon here and now thoughts, feelings and behaviours. Each one of us presents with our own defences structured to self protect and survive early unsoothed distress.

Early loss and trauma, painful in childhood, influences methods the individual creates to keep a sense of emotional and physical protection, in an attempt to make sense from chaos, like a band aid or plaster, holding together a wound actually needing major surgery. For many this defence is food and self comfort gained from eating. This in turn, becomes an eating problem, gaining and losing weight or the never ending circle of prevention, sapping physical and emotional energy. Food becomes the defence in order to keep helping the world inside be more comfortable than the world outside.

It is important to look at grief because if you are eating for self soothing or any of the things we are discussing in this book then you will be in some form of unfinished grieving process.

We experience grief in many forms. We face loss every day in one form or another, loss of time, the ageing process, loss of friends, changing circumstances, relationships, and so on, so many times we are traumatised by every day events.

Events Likely To Evoke Grief

There are many events in life both present day and historical, which are likely to evoke a grief response.

a) Present day death of a loved one.

b) Still births, miscarriages and termination of pregnancy.

c) Death of a loved significant other in the present day, which may be a trigger for past events, for example, separation, harm, and traumatic endings from childhood.

d) Breakup of a relationship.

e) Illness and injury to self or other, including pets, which are both past and present events.

f) Destruction of houses, office buildings, cities and countries witnessed first hand or in the media.

g) Loss of limb.

h) Loss of a beloved pet.

i) Loss of possessions like jewellery, memorabilia, and cars.

j) Change of space or quarters, moving house, translocation of work/home, all of which may bring up loss and interruption in life.

k) Boarding school or institutionalisation of some

kind where a child is separated from parents for a long period.

l) Forms of emotional deprivation and harm from childhood, emotional abandonment, unconscious messages sent by parents/carers who had covert or overt intention to harm.

m) A denial of reality by a parent and subsequently by oneself as an adult.

So much in life can bring forth the past unfinished business. For example a present day crisis may open doors in your consciousness where old grief and despair lie hidden, because in the past there was no way you could soothe the pain, or there was no one to help you pacify it or understand what was going on. As a child my life was desperately unhappy with what went on within the family. I felt that I could not turn to anyone and was often described as a miserable child or a 'moaning Minnie' by relatives and my mother. I witnessed violent behaviour from my father towards my mother; we repeatedly ran away from him and then returned only to go through the process again and again. I was a very depressed child and carried huge amounts of grief about what was going on. Each time we left my father I was taken out of school and put into another school somewhere else. Making friends became very difficult because a couple of weeks later or even months later I would be returned to my old school and put back into the class I had left without any explanation or discussion with either my parents or teachers. No one took the trouble to talk to me or find out what impact it had upon me.

Whenever we left home I left pets, toys and friends behind and on return things had of course changed. For most of my life I experienced a chronic anxiety and insecurity around people rarely expecting them to be interested in me or what I wanted.

When I reached forty my beloved dog died and suddenly I was plunged into a terrible grief and became very depressed, so much so I needed to take six months off work. In retrospect I recognise that what I was experiencing at that time was a releasing of the grief inside from the horrors of my childhood, triggered by the death of my dog. Although very sad about the loss of my dog the level of grief was unprecedented.

R.D. Laing says *'we maintain forgotten events whilst holding a repressed encoded representation'.*

In other words we hold the distress in our body if we do not allow ourselves to grieve fully for these traumatic events experienced at the time. Or if there is no way to have the hurt soothed when it happened the pain is internalised.

So often compulsive eating can be as a result of unresolved grief. Over eating is a way of holding down untapped and painful emotions from the past, mainly because we do not know how to soothe them any other way.

Whenever Pat told her mother she was upset about something, either in the family or from school or friends she would be given a sandwich, biscuit or something else to eat. Even worse she would be told that she was being silly and soft. Her story wasn't listened to or soothed with simple explanations, and cuddles.

There are symptoms of introverted loss issues which are brought into the here and now. By this I mean our behaviours reflect how we have dealt with loss in our younger days. For example, aspects of behaviour, ways of thinking and methods of dealing with emotions in the present day, some of which I have outlined below.

1. Maintaining a distance in case of any further loss.

2. Moving in and out of a relationship with the illusion of self protecting.

3. Steering clear of getting close to others so as to prevent the pain of loss.

4. Denial of events from the past and detachment in the present.

5. Self sufficiency with the act of being strong and pushing others away, behaviour due to early separation issues, for example boarding school, fostering and unavailability of parents.

6. Adoption which may affect feelings of trust and belonging issues.

7. Delayed and avoided grief of lost significant other.

8. Chronic grief that can be identified when the client tells of an inability to move forward in life. Feelings of emptiness and a void inside are described as part of the presenting problems.

9. Phobias used as a way of avoiding grief issues.

10. Guilt and Shame issues

11. Anger that may be long term towards a dead person.

12. Bitterness towards unidentified issues in life.

- Do any of the above touch on your own life?

- How have you dealt with major life issues?

- How did your parents deal with loss and major hurtful issues in life?

If issues of grief are left unresolved, it doesn't matter where or when it was in our history. If we have not allowed ourselves to grieve properly, then it may emerge the next time around. Also unresolved grief issues will take up a lot of your emotional energy just keeping it at bay. You will need to unravel it by moving through the following stages.

1. Accepting the loss as a reality

2. Entering into the emotions of grief

3. Acquiring new skills and adjusting to life.

4. Reinvesting energy into new ways of being.

Accepting the Loss as Reality

Here we go through a stage of denial and therefore slowly identify the loss as real, passing through the stages of shock and denial which are a healthy part of the slow realisation of the loss. We do this by looking back into our own histories and thinking about painful things that happened. We talk about them or write them down in the form of a diary to admit that they really happened. We find ways of opening up the past and bringing it into the present so that it can be acknowledged and healed. Of course there will always be scars but up to now we have been using only a small dressing to cover a gaping wound and once opened to the fresh air we may find ourselves feeling more energised and relaxed. We use a lot of psychological energy to suppress painful emotions. This makes life more difficult as we are functioning in our every day existence without that extra energy.

Entering into the Emotions of Grief

The grieving individual has to pass through the pain and emotion in order to heal, penetrating through fear in order to release emotions. Sometimes opening up painful issues from the past is frightening and we prevent ourselves from doing it by discounting the significance of what happened. We say things like 'Well its all in the past it doesn't matter now' or something along the lines of 'There is nothing to be done about things that happened in the past'. All of that is true but think of it this way; we know we can never change the past but we can change our feelings and attitudes towards it.

Adjusting to life and taking up new skills

Here the individual is faced to deal with daily reminders, coming to terms with feelings of regret and guilt, sleep disturbances, nightmares, moving backward and forward through the stages of denial and acceptance. For years I had nightmares about violence and aggression, I would wake up crying with fear often thinking I was being suffocated or some other terrible thing. Once I started to look into my dreams and accept them as some repressed fear from the past they began to subside because I was accepting the past as a bad time and my unconscious had been trying to tell me something. Once I began to write down my dreams I started to sleep better and went even further by talking to a therapist about them.

Reinvesting energy in life, making new relationships

This means saying a final farewell, leaving and letting go, rather than being left, taking on new permissions to go on living and dealing with the fears of new relationships. So many of us fail to live in the here and now with the people in our lives, we keep secrets, we don't let people we love know what is going on, all of this takes up our emotional energy and makes us tired. We have to let go of the painful issues from our past in order to move on in the here and now. Our relationships in the present and how we relate will be influenced by what we learned from the family we lived in as young children.

These tasks must not be over simplified and the first three tasks will be repeated over and over. Pathological grief occurs when the individual comes to a standstill on one or all four tasks, leading to delayed grief, avoidance of grief and chronic grief. This means grief is damaging us, emotionally affecting everything we do but we refuse to examine why. This is how we self harm by not allowing ourselves to feel the emotions that are necessary to move on. We suppress them in different ways, by deciding that it is silly to allow feelings out, or that it is shameful to feel feelings, or think that it is important to stay strong. We use differing methods to deal with these suppressed emotions, one is eating too much. Comfort eating and gaining weight will be a way of being big and strong in the face of adversity.

- Do you use food as a way of suppressing your emotions?

- What could have happened in your life that has left you with an unresolved grief issue?

If one is dealing with a here and now grief issue you will eventually move to the next stage. However with losses from the past, you may not have considered the grief as significant and may be unconsciously fixated at any one particular stage of grief.

When people fail to grieve they are left with *survivor difficulty*

> *To admit to the loss would then necessitate confronting a loss of part of oneself, so the loss is denied.*
>
> (WILLIAM WORDEN 1983)

He goes onto say that *'past losses and separations have an impact on current losses and separations and the capacity to make future attachments'*.

Bowlby described the loss of a loved one as the most painful emotion one can experience, not only is it painful but it is painful to witness.

- What did you witness as a child that remains unresolved within you?

Shelly came home from school one day to find the house in darkness, her father sitting quietly on the settee in the lounge. He told her that her mother had been hit by a car and had died in hospital. It had not occurred to him to call her from school or take her feelings into consideration. He went ahead with the funeral refusing to allow her to go or to discuss what happened. He brought down a great door on the whole thing. He never talked about it again and became a broken man who just continued with his life as if nothing had happened. Shelly was left to manage the loss of her mother alone, alongside the seeming loss of her father.

Research has shown that relationship patterns are carried forward, mostly as unconscious expectations of self other and life in general. When one has experienced trauma, separation, loss and abuse in childhood it will involve the need to grieve, loss of a safe attachment figure, loss of innocence, loss of sense of self, loss of trust, loss of self esteem, all of which lie hidden behind defences.

All loss is traumatic at various levels within the self, and thereafter if not dealt with, will influence personal development. It will influence the way we see ourselves and the way we believe others see us.

Your Personal Diary Entry

What grief have you experienced in your life which has had a bearing on who you are today?
Write down something that you have grieved for but perhaps you didn't think of it as something to grieve over.

_____

_____

_____

_____

_____

_____

_____

_____

_____

_____

_____

_____

_____

_____

_____

_____

_____

_____

_____

CHAPTER FOUR

•

HUNGER OF A
DIFFERENT KIND

What I am about to discuss are what is known as psychological hungers, first defined by Eric Berne (1970) so called because they reflect some of our basic needs, the first being **Contact**. This is the need for physical touch by other people. Contact can be received by hugs, hand-holding, pats, massage, or any other way you get physically touched. Greeting others with handshakes or hugs and kisses and showing happiness at the contact. Some elderly people who live alone can go days or weeks without having any physical contact at all, how do you think this would impact upon their well being?

The second is **Recognition hunger**; this is the need to be noticed, receive attention and acknowledgment which can only be supplied by another human being. It is a need for a sense of belonging, and feelings that other people know you are alive. This is why milk is not enough for infants; they also need the sound, smell, warmth and touch of mothering or else it may be that they fail to thrive and suffer from deprivation. Just as grownups do if there is no one to say hello to them. Recognition is given in the form of verbal strokes such as a simple nod, someone saying your name, hello, or giving you compliments or praise both for who you are and what you do. By the way it is OK to ask for recognition.

The third is known as **Incident** and here we have a need to experience anything that might be challenging, exciting, novel, or different. It is doing something out of the ordinary. When you are bored or feel life is dull, than you are experiencing a lack of incident in your life. There is negative unplanned incident, i.e. losing your car keys, getting into an argument with a friend, stubbing your toe, or bouncing a cheque. Examples of positive incident are vacations, parties, eating different kinds of food in restaurants, sleeping on a different side of the bed, meeting new people, going to an amusement park, seeing unusual places, and having a flashy car. However for whatever reason many people are afraid of change. This in itself will influence whether or not we seek new activities. How do you deal with change and does food prevent you from making changes?

The fourth is known as **Stimulus hunger;** where we have a need for sensation, arousal and input into five senses: sight, sound, smell, taste, and touch. Far from avoiding stimulating situations, as some people have claimed, most human beings seek them out. The need for sensation is the reason why roller coasters make money and why prisoners will do almost anything to avoid solitary confinement. Other examples of fulfilling this need are: bright colours, music, smells in a bakery, interior decorating, art galleries, also stimulating the mind by creating new ideas, and smelling flowers and laughing.

The fifth is **Structure hunger** where there is a need to make meaning, make sense of what is happening in our world and in our relationships in order to feel secure and safe. This is the need for time structure or what one does with his/her time from birth to death in order to avoid the pain of boredom. It is important to remember that as much as you plan your work time, it is as important to plan your play time. This need is fulfilled by having goals, keeping a calendar, attending classes, having a satisfying career and/or having one's own business. As the famous private detective Hercule Piorot says, 'Using the little grey cells'.

Finally there is the need to be aroused and reach a peak. This hunger can be met in different ways. Enthusiasm about life; watching or participating in sports, dancing, telling funny stories or jokes, having intimacy with other people, liking one's own femininity or masculinity, flirting, or body painting.

Dancing and Sex fulfill all six of these hungers at the same time

Think back now as to where you might be out of sync with some or all of the above.

- How do you get your contact with others?

- Do you want contact or avoid it?

- How do you get yourself noticed?

- Do you feel as if you belong?

- Do you give recognition to others if so how?

- Do interesting things happen to you?

- Do you make them happen or wait for things to happen to you?

- What stimulates you and gives you pleasure?

- What is your favourite colour, music, smell etc?

- How do you make yourself feel secure?

- Is structure important to you or are you disorganised is various aspects of your life?

- Are you structured in your self care?

- What are you enthusiastic about in your daily life?

- Do you have hobbies, what interests you?

- How are you intimate, do you share your thoughts, feelings and ideas with others?

- Do you allow others into your world?

When you reach the chapter on 'How to Change' I would advise you to refer back to this chapter reviewing your own structure hungers.

Communication

As a child you will have observed methods of communication within the family system. If communication was an important priority and those around you made themselves clear, acting in an empathic way and were supportive to each other, then you will have been listened to and your thoughts and feelings will more than likely have been taken into consideration. This will have had a positive influence in the way you express yourself and the way you listen to others. This does not have to be a perfect system merely good enough to show you the way to express your thoughts and feelings openly, and express your needs and wants truthfully.

However if within your family system the ways of communication were limited in terms of clarity then the modelling you witnessed will be limited also.

As a an only child Melton never felt seen or heard within his family, it was almost as if he wasn't there and only on rare and seemingly mechanical occasions was he acknowledged by the adults in his household. As an adult he would describe himself as being invisible around other people and it seemed that for him it was difficult to make himself seen and heard. Because of his low self-esteem he could not assert himself and continually reinforced this belief about himself through both his behaviour and his expectation of the other's response. Melton behaved in ways that maintained that pattern of not being seen or understood. How he communicated his needs or wants determined whether or not other people acknowledged him. He acted in a way that would retain his life position of believing that he was not important enough to get seen by others. He saw himself as being badly treated in relationships. One way or another either in his awareness or out of it he will have to change his method of communication because as a child he had been overlooked and missed by his family he now played the overlooked and missed behaviour pattern. He used food as a way of consoling himself but of course in a negative way he presented himself to the world as vulnerable through his weight. Although successful in his career he worked in the most part alone in his work with computers and felt a deep profound loneliness. Because of his early childhood experiences he found making himself seen almost impossible so his obesity, although obviously noticeable kept the real Melton invisible.

Sarah had a fear of other people being angry with her. Therefore she would temper her language to make sure that whatever she said wouldn't bring anger her way. She would say difficult things with a wide smile and her head slightly tilted to one side along with a little giggle thus giving a mixed message.

'I am telling you that I am angry but don't be angry back because I'm really a nice person'.

'I don't really mean what I am saying to you right now' and so on.

This mixed message would cause confusion between herself and the other person. In this behaviour pattern Sarah was giving the other person half the picture of her wants in her relationship with them, so that they would have to try to make sense of what she is saying in order to stay in contact with her. Perhaps Sarah as a child was afraid that if she asked for what she wanted the parents would leave her, reject or humiliate her in some way. Many of her friends would probably never know that Sarah was angry. They might see her as a person who lacked energy in terms of effort in the rela- tionship, in other words Sarah might be seen as a bit of a door mat or maybe even not accounted for at all because of her passivity.

On the other hand Sarah may have surround- ed herself with people who didn't express what they wanted clearly so that she never had to feel challenged by others in her life. As a child she had experienced a great deal of fear about others anger and because of her history she often got caught up in relationships where she was bullied or controlled and did not recognise let alone express how she felt about that. She used food to self soothe and hide her true feeling from the world and from herself. She would eat to fill the space created by her isolation from her true feelings of anger at the way she had been treated as a child.

Comfort eating

Over eating is a way of compensating for angry and upset feelings towards oneself and others. One is overwhelmed by emotion thus over eating, dieting and often self purging helps one feel in control of life, whilst at the same time feeling out of control around food.

I think it important to state here I am not only discussing the comfort eater, but also the compulsive eater and indeed anyone of you who have difficulty just losing weight and keeping it off. What are we doing that we cannot keep to a healthy weight and battle continually to maintain a reasonable weight? There is considerable pressure in just maintaining a reasonable weight for many of us, maybe not reaching the over 20's sizes but repeatedly fighting against it and having what feels like out of control, over indulgent moments which we feel helpless to contain.

Comfort eating, at its most extreme may be characterised, to a greater or lesser degree with spates of over eating followed by dieting, shifting from one diet to another in the hope of finding the right one. A diet that will be easy and give rapid results, often eating what might be termed 'something nice' or 'a reward' or used as a way of dealing with problems in life. Food should not be considered as a reward it should be something to fulfil a hungry space, a natural phenomenon. In reality the individual may not be eating badly but because of the constant cycle of dieting cannot see food in its reality. It maybe that the individual will go through periods of starvation in order to try to lose weight, moving from self denial then shifting to over indulgence. This is one of the marked signs of feeling out of control around food. Self purging by taking repeated doses of laxative after a period of over eating is often as a result of guilt. An individual, who is caught in a continuous cycle of dieting and over eating in the main, struggles with anxiety, depression, self hate and shame. They also experience anger, both at the world and at themselves.

Of course you the reader will know that being hard on oneself goes no way towards helping to end the problem.

• Are you hard on your self, if so how?

• Are you in a cycle of dieting and over eating?

All of this is linked with craving food as a replacement for something else. In the main we do not know what this is but it could be called an addiction to food. Many would describe it as an addiction to carbohydrates. It is widely researched that over eating is a way of covering up emotions. In the beginning, I believe that is true but as the years go on, it is more of a habit.

It is, of course, possible that you are addicted to carbohydrates just as one can become addicted to drugs, alcohol and smoking.

- Would you describe yourself as having an addiction or an addictive personality?

- When you crave something to eat what could you do instead?

- What is it you are craving for?

When our eating is out of control we are disowning our true feelings and quite possibly defending against shame, humiliation and rejection which means we have the urge to over adapt to the needs of others, trying to please, hiding oneself and ones own needs for fear that the other might be angry or displeased about us not considering them first. Of course, invariably the other person is completely oblivious to what is happening.

Redefining is a part of the way we invite others to stay attached to us or the way we protect against engulfment. This is a complex process. An individual will redefine in order to maintain some sense of inner security, feeling as if they are in control of what is happening around them.

When an individual redefines they are trying to keep the world safe but as a child when their reality was questioned they had to try and make sense of what was going on around them. A simple example of redefining is when you ask someone what they are **thinking** and they respond with something like "I am **feeling** upset". You might ask someone, "What are your plans for today?" They may respond with, "It looks like it might be a nice day".

Look for redefining in your communication with others.

Redefining simple means one will answer a different question than has been asked. We redefine in order not to feel or think about what is really going on. We make life easier for ourselves by doing this. If one is hurt by something often we avoid feeling that hurt by saying to ourselves.

'Well they didn't mean that, they were only saying or doing it because of this, or this'. In that way we do not have to face our own hurt.

Not everyone who is overweight has an eating disorder. When I talk about comfort eating I am using it as a link towards other eating issues for example: eating to soothe a part of oneself that seems unable to decide what is needed to deal with varying emotions like anger, sadness and fear. I am also looking at it as over eating in order to placate a part of oneself that is agitating or distressed.

When we discuss compulsive overeating we distinguish it with uncontrollable eating followed by feelings of guilt and shame and sometimes purging between bingeing and secret over eating.

What are the warning signs of compulsive eating? (Health education)

- Bingeing, or eating uncontrollably

- Purging by strict dieting, fasting, vigorous exercise, vomiting or abusing

- Using laxatives or diuretics in an attempt to lose weight

- Using the bathroom frequently after meals

- Preoccupation with body weight

- Depression or mood swings

- Irregular periods

- Developing dental problems, swollen cheek glands, heartburn and/or bloating

What are the signs of comfort eating, over eating and yo-yo dieting?

I prefer to use the term comfort eating which indicates one of the levels of compulsive eating, which stretches from the mild to the extreme. It is distressing because of the need to self soothe by using food. Some of the signs are listed below such as having a preoccupation with body weight, getting on scales each morning, and experiencing mood swings and depression. Eating to excess which causes one to be over weight, can come under the heading of compulsive eating, and yet it does not necessarily go along side purging and binge eating. However there may be some of this to a greater or lesser degree.

As a young woman Sarah would use laxatives on a regular basis in the vain hope that it would keep her weight down. In truth she was never hugely over weight but her self image indicated to her that she was. Sarah had never really considered what she was doing to be self harming, and a very damaging process to her digestive system. She told me that it gave her a sense of wellbeing to purge herself and had never considered it to be damaging. It is important to note that daily purging of the bowel is an irritant and will eventually damage the lining of the bowl possibly leading to cancer or ulcerative colitis etc.

➤ Mindless eating

This means to eat without thought or care in terms of hunger, or desire. It is merely a process of forgetting about oneself and what you might really want at the time. It is a process of forgetfulness about your own needs, and not taking time to consider the question of 'what do I really want?'

It is a major way of discounting yourself, you are failing to think about what you want or consider your own needs.

➤ Grazing throughout the day

Generally this is about looking for something to fill a space which is rarely to do with hunger, in fact it is more likely to be about having missed meals in some variable diet, not eating enough at regular meal times, so feeling deprived only to eat foolishly later. It is about looking in the fridge and cupboards for comfort.

Someone likened this process to spending money two or three pounds at a time, buying cheap or 'bargain items' but on a regular basis, imagining they are saving money. Instead of choosing carefully and buying quality, it would seem that in this instance they could accumulate a wardrobe full of clothes in the belief they had saved money. In terms of grazing we can fool ourselves we are not eating much only to have accumulated about three hundred or so extra calories in the day. We can then convince ourselves that we don't eat much but are eating a handful of raisins a roast potato, a spoonful of veg, a bit of meat off the joint as we carve and so on. Picking up a biscuit or finishing the baby's dinner.

> **Eating whilst preparing food**

This, in my experience is generally because one person, namely the main carer, is the person who provides the nourishment and the nurturing for others. It connects with the mindless eating but could also be to do with feelings of frustration. Preparing meals for others, dealing with caring for others, whilst trying to suppress ones own needs and desires. Eating unhealthily when putting your own needs at the bottom of the pile, because of feeling overwhelmed by your urge to care for those who look to you for their meals and basic care. It means picking at the food you are preparing, seemingly eating like the rest of the family but actually consuming almost a full meal just in its preparation.

What happens when you are dealing with cooking for others? What is lacking in your own life and how do you use food as a substitute. How do you take care of yourself whilst nurturing others?

> **Eating snacks after a large meal**

After dinner, not feeling satisfied and yet full and possibly bloated. This lack of satisfaction is not about hunger, it is about the craving, the unmet needs from the past,

and it is about some unfulfilled aspects of the self.
What is unfulfilled within you?
What do you really want?

To discover this you will need to look at what happened prior to your meal, what has happened during the day which may have been ignored by yourself about yourself? Look back at the events of the day.

➤ **Eating to fill a feeling of boredom**

How many of you go to the kitchen to fill an empty space or to fill time, especially in the evenings when time needs to be filled and yet there is a space inside that feels incomplete? Is there a space in you that seems insatiable? Look into your relationships, how do you communicate with those you love? Poor communicative abilities are often the reason we turn to food. What is missing in your life? Are you reliant upon others for your entertainment or your direction or are too many others reliant upon you for their happiness?

➤ **Skipping meals in order to save on calories**

Some dieters skip meals in the belief that they will be able to save calories, in fact they are seeking control but generally by the end of the day they will have moved to losing control, eventually giving in to hunger and need which seemingly can only be controlled with food and instant gratification.

➤ **Days of starvation**

Starvation is not an extreme, it is a fact that many dieters resort to. Not eating primarily is born of fear and panic at the weight gain that shows on the scales each morning. It is a resolution made on each individual day and will be too hard to sustain. The starvation urge for the compulsive eater is about trying to regain control of their eating but along with it comes the physical discomfort because the body goes into tortured process of eating itself, and with hunger comes nausea, headaches and tiredness all of which will be too hard to sustain for more than a few hours within the twenty-four hour period.

➤ Yo-Yo dieting

This is a repeated loss and regain of weight due to repeated dieting. This is a process where the dieter begins an extreme diet which they cannot sustain, losing some weight and then regaining it again. The weight loss can be a big one or small but this continued process is about an obsession with food. The yo-yo dieter thinks about food from the beginning of the day through to its end, planning and trying to control what can be consumed and what is bad or good about food. The dieter is affected by depression and tiredness due to the strain of trying to maintain an extreme diet, and eventually will return to what could be termed normal foods only to regain the weight.

We suffer from eating problems because of low self esteem. We rarely diet just to lose a bit of weight using healthy eating; we use methods that are about self denial and harshness of method. Eating issues are about imagining that life will improve in some way if only we could lose weight. If we were slim others might find us attractive, loveable or sexy etc. This in itself is about seeking approval and attention because of our dietary issue.

Compulsive eating along side compulsive dieting is about how life would be better if only we were slim. Our methods of getting slim however is about self harm and self deprivation in 90% of cases.

Dieting healthily is about losing weight slowly, eating sensibly and matching what is on the inside with what is outside.

Somewhere inside the compulsive eater is looking to control emotions and life itself through food. When you tell other people you are on a diet, (Which dieters do frequently) you are trying to let others know that you are in control of yourself and life, when in fact you are feeling completely out of control.

Compulsive eating, over eating and eating disorders per se, are about dealing with stress, coping with emotional upheaval, self doubt, anger, confusion, fear and low self esteem and poor self worth. High levels of anxiety, i.e. chronic anxiety, has always been there as a part of life and lies just below conscious awareness.

In all of the aspects above we need to look for how to deal with it all, and I wish there was one answer. In the past you have probably tried every diet there is, you will have been to slimming clubs, you will have used many forms of dieting all of which encourage self denial but all discount your own personal history.

A theme of most slimming clubs is to use what is called a cognitive behavioural method, or Neurolinguistic programming. In other words mind over matter. Using thinking rather than feeling to overcome the problem of food. Paul McKenna has the right idea with his methodology in his book 'I Can Make You Thin' and I like what he offers. However, although sound, especially his advice about eating slowly and chewing your food well, laying down the knife and fork between every mouthful, thinking about what you want and so on all excellent advice. Read his book and use it alongside or after reading this one. He states that if you stick to his diet you will lose weight, I could not agree more, however that would apply to any diet you are on. *If you follow this diet you will lose weight,* what is missing is the plain fact of why. He states clearly that he is surprised at the number of people whose weight gain coincides with a traumatic incident from the past and recommends that you get help for that. I support that whole heartedly and urge you to find professional help with your personal trauma in the process of reading this book. There are many therapists and counsellors out there to turn to for help.

What drives you to over eat? What is the process in your life you are dealing with on a daily basis? In all the slimming clubs I ever attended I was never asked the simple question, 'Will you tell your story?' or 'Tell us about your inner struggle?'

Of course I understand that time is limited also the teachers in the groups are not trained to deal with the powerful emotions that are lying dormant and so often require someone to listen and encourage the grief which lies beneath the urge to over eat, or to eat badly. In the main none of the dieting organizations look at why, they do not indicate that the past is of any significance. I don't believe we can change how we eat unless we are aware of the pain of the past, find where the crooked penny is in the stack which sent us off balance? Where did we begin the process of feeling guilty, or shamed enough to want to die? Why do we self harm and seem unable to change it?

Frankie told me that her body hurt so much she could not bear the idea of living to an old age. She was tired of the constant struggle to get through each day repeating the negative pattern of fighting food, disgusted at her own body, and the shame about failing to lose weight, experiencing herself as out of control around food. When we looked back into her history she described the care she received as erratic, describing her mother as unable to sustain loving care for any length of time. Her mother had soon tired of Frankie's neediness and could not maintain closeness for long. Of course when we examined aspects of her mother's history it was more horrifying than Frankie's so what else could be expected? What did emerge was Frankie struggled to sustain long term care of her self, growing bored of her own neediness after more than a couple of days. Once she realized this she started to recognise how to love and care for herself on a regular basis. This was something that required time to change. In essence this would mean she had to be patient with herself in a way her mother hadn't been.

In my experience I have found both professionally and personally in some cases there has been an unboundaried process around food which becomes a way of life. Over eating is done because the individual has forgotten or indeed never learned how not to do it, never learned to think about what they are doing or what is behind this need for food without hunger. It is like taking risks without checking for the safety aspects, jumping out of a plane without a parachute, putting a hand into an unguarded fire, walking across a motorway, running across railway lines. Over eating is just as hazardous and we wouldn't do it and yet we over eat, become obese and this in turn causes many health problems, but we still do it. Is there a part of us that wants to die, but maybe doesn't really want to commit suicide? Like smokers who continue to smoke knowing that it might eventually kill them? Is 'might' the operative word here? Or are we secret rebels that take risks without thinking of the consequences?

- Why would I continue to do something I know is bad for me?

- What is that about? Do I want to die?

- Am I looking for a way out of the life I live?

- Can I consider myself a rebel in life?

I had a friend who one could consider to be a very conservative person, always smart, very successful in life and yet he would continue to break the rules whilst driving his car. He would often refuse to wear a seat belt, park on double yellow lines and steal the occasional book from the library and even a book shop. Whenever confronted on this behaviour he would say things like 'Who would care?' 'Why shouldn't I?' or 'What does it matter?' and so on. He was what could be call a sweetheart rebel, charming and fun to be with and yet sabotaging his life by taking risks in the legal stakes, almost as if he just wanted to push against society. I know this example might seem extreme but it might be worth looking at your own rebellious streak, I think you might find that you have one or maybe two.

Those who suffer from over eating problems are generally fully aware that they have a problem and are, in the main, conscious of how others view them. They carry a secret sense of shame, of being seen as 'lazy' 'greedy' or 'lacking in self control.' They hear from so many that all they need to do is 'Go on a diet' or 'Just eat healthily' People who are compulsive eaters all too often feel out of control and know what the dangers are, just as a smoker knows that smoking kills yet possibly fails to acknowledge it. Compulsive eaters recognize the dangers of diabetes, heart conditions, blood pressure and high cholesterol amongst other things and yet make a choice to discount the consequences. Indeed many have some form of medical condition to deal with at the same time. Might I venture to say that when we rebel in this way we hurt only ourselves? I know that so often I battled with myself about wanting to eat even though I had no hunger, in the past, when in the midst of a struggle I would say things like "Who cares?" and "Why shouldn't I?" as if society or someone out there was watching and waiting for me to make a mistake. It is difficult sometimes to know that having a healthy weight is for me not for anyone else. This is sometimes what compulsive eaters forget.

Many of us eat to calm ourselves down, to help us deal with emotional upheavals. We eat when we are bored, lonely or depressed. We eat when we are angry and don't know how to deal with that.

- How many of you look to the fridge to give you the answers to your problems or for something to do?

- How many wander around the house reflecting on how to prevent yourself from pushing food into your mouths?

- How many of you graze throughout the day?

Remember we eat to soothe and satisfy some unmet need or some turmoil in side that is the result of some thing seemingly, uncontrollable happening outside ourselves. Eating fills a gap caused by loneliness, generally a deep unfulfilled loneliness that makes friends and family impotent to help. Somewhere in life we have abandoned the real self and now present a false self to the world.

We eat for comfort when we feel life is out of control, and when *we* are out of control. Eating recharges us when we feel tired but it doesn't last, so we do it again and again in the vain hope that it will. The irony is that over eating also makes us feel more tired and bloated, but at least we have a temporary respite from the realities of life, albeit short lived.

Over eaters can eat quite normally in front of others, and will generally eat small amounts at parties because they are conscious of other people's eyes upon them.

In the main the extra food will be eaten alone and sometimes in the middle of the night.

Over eating is a way of dealing with self hate, guilt, anger, sadness and anxiety.

- How many of you will be thinking of food throughout the day, the next meal, what to have, counting
  calories or following some other dietary system?

- How many of you will continue to eat after feeling
  full, and will be yo yoing with meal times and dieting throughout the year?

- When you have turned to the fridge and its con-
  tents for support, do you feel any better?

What does it mean to crave?

It means to have an intensely strong desire for something, to yearn and long for that something. Where there
are food issues then there are cravings for various foods,
chocolate, salted nuts any thing that constitutes carbohydrates. There have been studies about being addicted
to carbohydrate. It certainly feels true that certain foods
never seem enough. For some, one slice of cake isn't
enough, gradually, although battling with the internal
distress of should I /shouldn't I, along with self deprecation and self loathing, a whole cake if unattended can
be consumed. Many people buy cakes for the family but
before it's even seen by any one it has been consumed
by its purchaser. As sad as that is, it is a common phenomenon for many. One piece of chocolate from a bar
rewrapped and put away for later is an impossible task
for the compulsive eater, or the binge eater.

- Have you ever eaten something that was originally
  bought for the whole family?

- Do you have a supply of crisps or snacks bought for so called 'visitors' but they are eaten by yourself when alone?

Those who suffer from eating problems are generally fully aware that they have a problem and are, in the main, conscious of how others view them. They carry a secret sense of shame, of being seen as 'lazy' 'greedy' or lacking in 'self control'. They hear from so many that all they need to do is 'go on a diet' or 'just eat healthily'

Body Image

When you over eat you use weight as a block to close-ness and relationships, and probably feel sad that relationships are unsatisfying. Being overweight is a perpetuation of yourself not being good enough and feeling ashamed of your weight and trying to hide your poor self esteem by eating. Food helps you to cope with some of your feelings but at the same time you are caught in a cycle of self loathing and eating. You may have a longing to be loved yet also recognise that you might be making yourself unlovable.

Many people who use food in a way to self harm, all too often require validation from others, but use food as a way to overcome that need of affection and recog-nition. It is a cycle of self hate and disgust and yet it is also about being out of control. It is an individual's own internalised image of their personal appearance that matters. If you have a poor body image you will consider yourself as unattractive to others, however this image of the self is linked to how well you percieve yourself as a whole, if you have low self esteem then this will be a part of the whole. In the main an individual who has a strong sense of self worth is more likely to accept their body as it is. It is a true saying that beauty is in the eyes of the beholder and what is attractive to one person may be less attractive to another. How we see ourselves will be distinctly related to our own self esteem. I remember a friend from years ago who repeatedly bemoaned how she had bad breath and was very conscious of anyone getting too close in case they smelt her breath. I had been close and on no occasion did her breath smell bad. She had been to the doctors and had had thorough examinations of her digestive system, which was healthy. She had visited her dentist on numerous occasions, and he reasurred her repeatedly. What did emerge was her opinion of herself was very low and she expected to be rejected in most aspects of her life because of terrible physical abuse by her mother who seemed to hate her. She used this unconscious process of having bad breath to keep others at bay. Keep others away before they got too close. Keep distant in case they saw that she was not a nice person as her mother had so frequently stated because then they would reject her. Her mother had stolen from her any grain of hope that she was loveable, so she had found a way to protect herself from any further percieved rejection.

Self Esteem

Self worth or self esteem is about how much you love, like and respect you. It is something that develops over time.

• How many of you have just settled for a certain type of relationship?

• How many of you drifted into your marriages or your long term relationships?

• Was it what you really wanted? Was this person really who you wanted?

• How many of you felt flattered by the attention someone gave you and felt so pleased to have some-one (anyone) you went along with the process, only to find that into the relationship you were back within the shadow of your criticising or rejecting family situation.

Whilst working as a health visitor many years ago I was surprised to find how many of the couples I vis-ited with children and new babies weren't actually in love. Many women confessed to me how they believed no one would ever want them. When they did meet someone who showed an interest, they were so afraid to lose them. They decided that it would be OK to settle as it might be their last chance. I must emphasis that I have also spoken to men who have said similar things about their relationships. Drifting into a mar-riage in a passive way, flattered by the fact that some-one actually wanted them enough to go out with and even marry. However women are more likely to have wanted to escape from negative family situations only to find themselves repeating history. Women who have watched their mothers abused by their fathers, women who have low self worth because of lack of recognition within the family, women who are looking for some way to escape from their life as it was, move into relationships that would seem better on the surface but later develop into a replay of the past.

This of course is all to do with how we value ourselves and the extent of our self-esteem. If self esteem and self worth are low because as a child you were undervalued or treated as a worthless object within the family system, or your feelings, thoughts and even sense of being there was discounted and overlooked, then how can you experience yourself as valuable?

As I stated earlier we first have to be valued to feel valuable.

Perhaps if someone, for example a teacher, places a value upon you or someone at work sees you as worth having around, then that in itself might trigger the beginning of some insight into feeling valuable. Perhaps you can begin to imagine that you are worthwhile? Being valued by someone else leads you toward feeling important.

Remember I said our sense of self-value originally comes from the carers around us.

However if you devalue yourself enough to stay in unhappy relationships or negative situations then you need to ask yourself why.

Placing a high value upon yourself means high self esteem and this in itself will help you to overcome the need to use food to compensate for lack of love and self worth.

- Do you allow yourself to be swept along if someone seems kind and asks you do something for them?

- Have you gone along with things you didn't want to do because you had been asked?

- Have you gone along with something just because you liked the person who was asking and felt afraid that you may lose them if you didn't comply?

- Has the attention of the other person caused you lose sight of your self?

- Have you been swept along in a love affair just because you were grateful for the attention?

Through maintaining the negative situations an individual can in some way preserve a false sense of security. As I mentioned earlier being in an unhappy marriage with a partner who treats you badly might be familiar and it is possibly all you know.

Similarly, being in a job that is not satisfying or where you are unnoticed , looking after others and ignoring your own needs or maybe not even recognising what your own needs are and why you stay in negative situations, remaining in a marriage where you are unappreciated or a relationship where your partner puts you down and so on?

- Why do you stay in uncomfortable situations?

- How do you use food to compensate?

You do it because there is safety in familiarity this gives a false sense of security even whilst feeling the hurt and distress. You can cope with it because you are unsure as to whether you deserve anything better. It may not even occur to you that you can have something better. Although throughout this chapter I have posed questions as food for thought, below I offer you the opportunity to notice how, through owning aspects of yourself, you may begin to move forward, and hopefully where you use food to self soothe you will begin to see why and change it.

Once we understand why we do something it gives us the opportunity to change.

- Do you remember how you first got recognition? Picture the scene and allow yourself to remember how that felt and what influence it had on you.

- How do you value yourself and what do you have to do to keep the feeling?

- How do you devalue yourself in relation to others?

- How do you cover up your sense of inadequacy?

- What would you change about yourself if you had a magic wand, and if you could change it what difference would it make in your life.

- What do **you** need to change in **yourself** in order to change the way **you** view relationships? This may be a belief about yourself, others or life in general.

- Do you have the urge to see it all as someone else's fault when things go wrong in your life?

- What would you have to own in you? What would you have to take responsibility for in the way you are in relation to others?

Shame

Many of us are ashamed of feeling shame, and terrified of being shamed by someone else. Shame is an unbearable feeling. It is a combination of multiple emotions, fear, humiliation and worthlessness, and it includes the terror of abandonment from childhood.

A deep physical pain accompanies shame and once recognised the individual will do anything to avoid feeling it in the future. As a way of hiding shame they may present as defensive, angry and will deny any feelings because of the painful internal humiliation.

Shamed based issues begin in childhood, statements such as 'big boys don't cry' and 'you are a baby', fairly common you might say, however repeated over time along with other humiliating condemnations from the important parental figures or older siblings or school are like Chinese water torture. They will make a damaging mark upon your personality. Over eating is a way of keeping shame at bay and yet is shaming in itself.

As we grow we internalise the early shaming statement made by the carers

'I am a fool, what an idiot'
'What a dick head I am'

'I can't do anything right'
'I can't be trusted'
I am so stupid'
I am so clumsy'

How you do this is to change the language slightly.

You will notice that the adult you has changed what was directed at you as a child and internalised it as true.

'You are a fool, what an idiot you are'
'You are a dick head'
'You cannot do anything right'
You can't be trusted'
'You are so stupid'
'You are so clumsy'

- Think of some of the negative messages from childhood which you may have taken on board and now used to shame yourself before someone else does it.

All of this is an indication of low self esteem, but it will be well hidden from others and lies just below conscious awareness. Often it is far too painful to face your history because you have to feel the full horror of your original critic where shaming has been used as a way to control.

We see ourselves as we were seen by those powerful others from our childhood, there are often conflicting messages for example:

'You are too soft' meaning you are a sucker for others but then comes the conflicting message

'You are such a selfish sod'.

'You need to eat everything on your plate'

Conflicts with 'you are greedy and your eyes are bigger than your belly'

- Can you identify some conflicting messages in your own history?

In the shame wound the individual is continually providing a stream of negative messages, internally undermining themselves, putting themselves down. Mainly before anyone else can do it.

Doing it to oneself may have provided a strong element of self control.

- If you are saying derogatory things to yourself ask why?

- Is it to protect you against humiliating feelings should anyone else call you stupid or think you are stupid etc?

It is possible to shame oneself without anyone else knowing. Shame is about being ashamed. 'I am bad'; 'I am hopeless' etc is a form of self protection and eases the chance of anyone else saying it. If you say it to yourself or to someone else you feel more in charge of that part of you. To feel ashamed is to feel bad. Often this goes along with feeling like a bad person; somewhere you are saying that if you really knew me you would see I am stupid, bad, ugly etc'.

Shame is about **being** wrong, not **doing** wrong' it is a fundamental aspect of the self which has manifested from childhood.

- Try saying if you really knew me you would see that I am ....bad, ugly, stupid, loveable or beautiful etc

- You add on what you think someone would see in you.

Toxic shame has been described as induced in child-hood through child abuse, sexual, incest, or physical abuse which violates the child's psyche. The child feels the shame the abuser refused to accept as their own. The adult who hurt or shamed you has succeeded in shifting their own shame about what they are doing onto you as a child. Is that fair?

Your Diary Entries

Do you put yourself down?
Do you criticise yourself a lot?
If so, how and why do you do that?

_____

_____

_____

_____

_____

_____

_____

_____

_____

_____

_____

CHAPTER FIVE

•

WITHDRAWING AS A DEFENCE

Dissociation is the disconnection from full awareness
of self and time and/or external circumstances

It is quite normal to withdraw or dissociate, we go into a trance like state. Sometimes when we are tired or bored our mind wanders, we go off in our heads to a more interesting place or thought than what we are experiencing at the time. We can lose ourselves in a book or something on the television. Time passes and we haven't realised that we have been off somewhere.

Dissociation is a common phenomenon, it means simply to withdraw from the stresses of the here and now into a world inside your head. Children dissociate more readily than adults and will do so when experiencing trauma. When a child faces abusive behaviour from adults or has to deal with frightening experiences, they will flee into a safer place in their heads. For many of those who have been sexually abused it is recorded that they move into some fantasy world where they are safe or protected by some imaginary circumstances. Perhaps an individual needed to cut off from the external environment in order to survive the abuse. This becomes a defensive pattern that continues on into adulthood it becomes a way out of painful emotional experiences. Post traumatic stress is a form of dissociation when someone goes through a traumatic experience, like a road accident or a near death incident; they will go through a level of dissociation. It is therefore easy to see that when a child experience some form of trauma like physical or sexual abuse or lives in a frightening environment, then they will readily use the dissociation to escape from the situation.

I am introducing the idea of dissociating because, in the main, when we use food to self soothe or suppress emotions we are moving into the realms of cutting off from the reality of the moment. It is a form of moving away from the here and now and hiding. I am suggesting that mindless eating, compulsive eating and comfort eating are a form of dissociating from the reality of the here and now.

What happened in childhood for someone to be afraid to love or get close?

Below are some of the recognised separation anxiety issues in childhood. These issues are the seeds that cause the detachment, dissociation and/or need to control how to be or not to be in relationships. An individual brings into the present the defence mechanism that is avoidance of intimacy and the fear of the loss of it. Defences or script patterns are formed as a way of preventing the re experience of the pain of loss. Some of which are outlined below.

- Increased danger risks   not being wanted, wrong sex,

- Fear for survival   family scapegoat, outsider

- Threats to abandonment   abandonment itself

- Threats of suicide by a parent   actual suicide of one parent

- Anxious mother/Parents   child takes care of parents feelings

• Child overburdened with responsibility	'no one there' for the child
• Detached carers/alcoholic, drugs	unavailable, unstructured, and a chaotic system of care
• Lack of comfort and support	survival anxiety
• Violence and abuse	fear of death
• Loss of a parent/parents	sent away, fostered, boarding school

A self destructive process

This process of substituting food is a legacy, inherited from the family system and the behaviours of the family, not just our own parents but their parents before them. Each parent in the main tries to improve upon the parenting style they have experienced before. How many of us as parents have uttered the words I want to be different from my mother/father?

If as children we fail to get our basic needs met or if for some reason we have to learn that our needs don't count because the parent sees their own needs as more important, we will be affected through into adulthood and consciously or unconsciously try to compensate for that.

With a parenting style that is discounting and neglectful of the needs of a child, that child may grow up seeing themselves as no good or not good enough to be cared about, unlovable, unattractive and worthless etc, this in turn will of course affect self esteem. People who are emotionally and physically neglected learn to live with scarcity, and thus will have to find some other means of getting their own needs met. This may be through staying close to someone by suppressing what they want and going along with what the other person wants. It may be that the individual will grow up being secretive about getting their needs met and often this is where food comes in. There is also a huge element of shame when a child has been neglected in their need for love and care.

Over eating is a way to self soothe; it is a way to deal with the internal conflict that is a result of external disharmony. It is a way to control the external world that impinges upon the emotional self. Eating is a way of expressing the internal pain onto the external self, demonstrating distress whilst maintaining a sense of normality, which is not always obvious to the onlooker. The outside world if it so desired, could see the internal suffering manifested because the obese person is demonstrating their distress for all to see. The more the weight, the more obese the more distress is being shown. Sympathy however is not something forthcoming from the public arena. Usually ridicule and impatience are the general rule of thumb.

Many over eaters do not exhibit huge weight gains; merely stay on the fringe battling to maintain some reasonable weight, generally overweight but not so that some one would be pointing the finger.

Self deprecation leading to eating

Very often the individual, who compulsively eats for whatever reason, will go against themselves, experiencing an internal battle about whether to eat or not, when this is happening there seems to be no other option open to them. This internal struggle will be painful and there will be extreme bouts of emotional upset during this process.

I want something to eat, although I have just eaten so cannot be hungry, but I do want something else. Perhaps I am still hungry?
*Internal voice; No **you** don't, you aren't hungry! How can **you** want something else to eat?*
I do want something to eat, I just fancy something nice. I need something and will feel better when I have had a packet of crisps and some cheese crackers.
*Internal voice; No **you** don't need it.*
Why shouldn't I eat? What does it matter anyway?
Who cares? I don't care if I am fat or get fat so what!!

That 'You' voice in your head is trying to help but is not strong enough to contain you or indeed know how else to help. So although it argues with you it cannot offer you a better solution. This is what has to change.

This is only a tip of the iceberg to the internal strife when dealing with food even without hunger. When an over eater wants food they are not really sure whether they feel hungry or if they are just driven to eat. Most times the compulsive eater does not know the difference between feeling hungry and any other emotional feeling that may need satisfying in a different way.

Most of what happens is the repeated anger that is turned inwards, turned upon oneself because it is safer to be angry at ones own body, feelings, behaviours and looks than it is to be angry with someone for hurting you, for being cruel or thoughtless. It is easier to turn rage upon oneself in the form of guilt or seeing oneself as greedy, selfish and useless than it is to confront those who treated one with disdain, those who bullied you as children, and those who had little or no regard for who you were as a child.

You use food as a way of pushing down your painful emotions; some of you fear reprisal if daring to criticise or confront someone you love with anger or sadness about things that may have happened either in the past or in the here and now.

Sometimes our adult children hurt us but we refrain from telling them because we do not want to lose them. We do not tell friends that they have discounted us or hurt us in some way because we are afraid to lose them. We don't tell our loved ones their actions are selfish or dismissive of us because we are afraid to lose them. Sad as it may seem this process does stem from childhood when we were afraid to let our parents know they had been uncaring or selfish or abusive or aggressive in their handling of us. Why would we be afraid of letting our parents know what we felt?

Because there was a very real risk of abandonment, we were dependant upon them for our care, indeed, our very survival. It was better to have poor parenting than no parenting at all.

- When you are thinking about your own process listen to what you say to yourself

- Are you having an internal struggle with voices inside?

- Do you quarrel with yourself about whether to eat or not between meals?

Your Personal Diary Entries

How do you fight with yourself when it comes to eating?
Write your thoughts and feelings here.
Are you your worst critic?
Do you fear losing someone you love if you tell them you are upset?

_____

_____

_____

_____

_____

_____

_____

_____

_____

_____

_____

_____

_____

CHAPTER SIX

•

SYMBIOSIS

Symbiosis means seeking to repeat history within our relationship in order to feel more secure because of the familiar outcome.

We can say that in a symbiotic relationship two people act as one, one person over adapts to stay within the relationship with another. Speaking for the other, ending each other's sentences. For example, sometimes two people cannot make a decision about what to do or where to go.

Paul	Shall we go out somewhere? I am bored.
Jennie	OK where do you want go?
Paul	I don't know where do you want to go?
Jennie	I'm not bothered you decide.
Paul	I don't know either I just know I don't want to stay in.
Jennie	Shall we go for a walk?
Paul	Don't fancy a walk.
Jennie	What about the cinema?
Paul	Don't really fancy the cinema anyway there's nothing worth seeing.
Jennie	Shall we go out for a meal?
Paul	We can't afford to spend money of a meal out.

And so it goes on, Paul wants Jennie to be responsible for what they do, but he cannot accept her options and he really doesn't know what he wants, on some level neither does he want to take responsibility for what happens in case it isn't the 'right' thing to do. She on the other hand is desperately trying to please him.

- Do you recognise any of these patterns of behaviour?

- Can you think of some of your own situations?

As children we instinctively learn how we can improve situations for ourselves when we are around adults. Where there is disharmony a child will learn how to keep themselves safe. They will perhaps learn how to stay quiet and in the background in order to stay out of what is going on with the parents or between parent and other siblings. They may however also act out in some situations, drawing negative attention to themselves. Negative attention is sometimes better than none. Maybe a child witnesses how the parent gets angry with an older sibling and will then work out that it's best to behave in a different way in order to please the parent. Maybe they have learned that the best thing to do in this household is to play in a corner and ask for very little. These are the ways we learn to stay in a relationship.

- You might want to ask yourself what you did as a child to fit into the environment you were brought up in.

In other words as a child I might suppress aspects of myself to stay close to a parent, for example I may quickly learn how to adapt to the needs of my mother in order to stay safe. I might also recognise deep down inside that some aspects of me are not acceptable to my parent/carers so I instinctively try to suppress these parts of me.

Transactional Analysis psychotherapy describes symbiosis as two or more people behaving as if they are one. They come together in their behaviour to form a single person. An easy example of this is when a few people are in a room and one of them states, perhaps a few times, "is it hot in here, is anyone else hot?" but does nothing to change the situation.

Eventually one person will respond by saying something a long the lines of

"I will open a window". Someone takes care of the other person's need without having been asked directly. These people do not need to know each other. At its most extreme you may also recognise couples who dress the same, even grow to look alike.

On a more significant level a mother has a fraught and difficult relationship with the father of the child. She is often perceived to be unhappy by the child who decides, through both perception and intuition, that the mother needs to be looked after. She does this by being a good girl, helping and trying to please the mother in order to make her smile and be happy in the child's company. She must do this at some cost herself, not worrying her mother with any problems, all in order to try to meet her mother's needs. Of course as any observer will note the mother's needs cannot be met other than by a change in the relationship to the husband but as children we cannot comprehend this logic

A healthy symbiosis is between mother and child when the mother is able to take care of her own needs whilst taking care of her young child's. Instead of looking to the children to meet her needs, she will look outward to either her own parents or her partner, i.e. the father of the child or members of her family, for her essential support.

A further example of healthy symbiosis is where someone is ill or disabled or mentally ill or has a learning disability, thus there will be a need to have some of their needs anticipated, this could also be described as a healthy dependency.

Food can fill the gap that has been left in childhood, the relationship with food can be considered symbiotic, for example eating will fill the space from a time when there was no where to go and no form of comfort given to a child who was severely stressed. Food then becomes a substitute for the absence of care and attention. A child feels there is no space for her in the family when s/he cries or wants to be picked up or sit on the parent's knee, instead they are given a cake or biscuit or maybe not acknowledged at all.

Self soothing

Self soothing is how we deal with stress using methods of looking after ourselves when we are feeling anxious, sad and angry. When we feel distressed about something, for example a relationship issue, some problem with work, something to do with someone you love. When you are in conflict with another, mainly someone you care about, and you feel you have let them down or they are angry with you.

- How do you calm yourself?

- How do you cope with the internal disquiet, anxiety or turmoil?

- How as children did your parent soothe you when you were distressed, hurt or angry?

There are many methods. Some from the good-enough parenting style for example. A child falls down outside and bangs his/her knee and cries, then runs in to the parent/parental figures and they put their arms around him/her giving a big cuddle. They examine the hurt area and soothe it by putting on a plaster or kissing it better. The child then runs out to play again feeling soothed by the care and carries on. He or she has internalised this care and each time s/he is distressed, gets hurt or feels afraid s/he knows s/he can run to the carer and will receive adequate amounts of attention. Gradually over time the child learns that in order to self care one must stop and listen to the hurt and then find some way to self soothe.

For those of us who have problems with self care, over eating or self harming there have been other methods of care given, or lack of.

The child falls down and gets hurts, then runs in to the carer/parent. This time the carer shouts something, accusing the child of being careless. S/he may get pushed away or even smacked for being clumsy. S/he may be laughed at and shown up for being soft. Whenever this child feels hurt, anxious or afraid what do you think they will do with themselves?

They are likely to internalise that method of care, by being hard on themselves, calling themselves stupid, clumsy or silly. S/he will push his or her feelings to one side and ignore the distress no matter how minor or major, soothing in the negative method they were taught as a child. So having been discounted in times of stress s/he will discount as an adult under stress.

Too often the methods the compulsive eater uses are destructive, and manic. There is a panic inside which has to be calmed and for some the only way is eating. Pushing food in is a way of dampening down the emotion that threatens to overwhelm.

Many methods of self care are the internalised technique used by the original carers for example, bullying, unforgiving statements which one carries in one's head, demanding and harsh attitudes along with destructive behaviours used by the original carer.

The only way through this process is to learn how to self love, and be somewhat self indulgent, learning to deal with self limitation whilst staying away from self denial which has been one of the damaging factors in childhood development.

We are a product of the environment we were brought up in and yet there will also be genetic factors influencing how we respond and also which way we go in dealing with problems in our life. Where our methods are limited or poor or harsh then we have to relearn new ways.

A parent failing to give adequate care within a dysfunctional family, for example in a case of sexual and physical abuse, where there have been discounting processes between the parent and child or other siblings, all will evoke huge amounts of distress. We all know of the child who has been sexually abused by a neighbour or family member telling a parent only to have it denied or rebuked. We will continue to give ourselves the same inadequate care. A child quickly learns that if they disclose any problems to a parent the parent might only see it as the child's fault.

- How do you cope with the internal disquiet, anxiety or turmoil?

- How as children did your parent soothe you when you were distressed, hurt or angry?

- What is your own manner of self care?

- Do you treat yourself as you were treated?

Self Harm

Self harming is a way of dealing with painful and distressing situations. Bizarre as that sounds, the individual may feel comforted by taking control of the pain by *doing something* to hurt what they can see in order to give the distress some tangible meaning. Generally it is because they are unable to tell others what is going on inside. Doing harm to oneself is a way of dealing with unhappy aspects in life, things that may be overwhelming, anger, sadness, despair, loss, grief, self hate and guilt.

Visible self harming like, cutting, doing drugs are the more obvious ways, however, smoking, abuse of alcohol and overeating are self harming too. Long term chronic abuse of smoking, alcohol and obesity will eventually kill. In my view all of these are ways to commit suicide by harming the body over long periods of time. Perhaps not quite as clear cut as the action involved of slashing wrists or taking an over dose or inhaling carbon monoxide.

Most of us fear death and therefore to take a proactive role in dying would need a different mental attitude and if I asked anyone who smoked heavily or did drugs or over ate to the point of obesity would they see it as a way of committing suicide? I doubt it. By self harming in the ways I have mentioned it somehow puts death out of the remit of suicide. Putting death somewhere in the future and out of control makes it less feasible to be about committing suicide.

Many people carry weight until they reach old age but may have a lifetime's struggle with food and life in general. Smokers often say that their fathers smoked all their life until they reached ninety, he wasn't trying to commit suicide was he?

However, by carrying on a chronic relationship with something that may kill means it is all about chance, and a daily emotional struggle against life.

In Transactional Analysis psychotherapy we talk of Hamartic scripts. Script simply refers to an unconscious belief system which drives us forward and this is called a life script. It is about having made some important decisions about our self, other people and life in general. There are many kinds of scripts but the Hamartic script is a damaging and negative way of life and generally the individual with a self harming script has an unconscious and conscious drive to hurt themselves, someone else or simply wants life to end.

James was physically abused as a child by his father and unprotected by his mother or other members of his family, as a small boy he decided that he must be worthless and hateful for his father to hit and hate him so much, whilst at the same time in his heart he knew that how he was treated was wrong and shocking. So he decided that they were not OK, whilst at the same time believed there was something wrong with himself. As James grew up, his opinion of himself and his family reflected his view of the world, himself and other people, in the main he felt angry with others but this did not show in his behaviour, merely in his view of the way things were. He had very little time for people, felt unable to trust them and although successful in his chosen career he was hiding a deeply held belief about himself, which he instinctively kept hidden from others. He did this by keeping himself apart, not letting himself get close. He was also very afraid of having children in case he would carry on as his father had done.

James used food as a way of soothing the angst feelings inside, although he wasn't overweight he spent a lot of his time pushing to the limit in the gym and jogging. He did not have time for relationships and abused his body by drinking too much as well as binging or starving on a regular basis. His joints began to suffer because of his haphazard methods of self care.

James told me that he found life to be a terrible struggle and often wished himself dead.

People cope with life in many and varied ways, by giving you examples of another person's issues and histories I am wanting to highlight the significance of finding your personal links with the past that now impinge upon your present day reality.

I urge you to think, is there any part of you that wants out of life?

For some of us there are certain aspects of our make up that may hold as part of the script I mentioned earlier, a get out clause. This simply means what we call in Transactional Analysis an open window or an escape hatch, where we can say something to ourselves like,

'If life gets bad enough I can always kill myself or hurt myself, or maybe hurt someone else or kill someone else, or perhaps go crazy.'

Only very recently I was talking to a friend who felt rather down, she owned that being ill might mean that someone else would take care of her. Granted it was only for a brief moment she felt like this, but it shocked me to think that even now she could still think that being ill, or ill enough to die, would shift her out of her lifetime struggle with food.

Think if you have an escape hatch open. Sometimes being ill, going crazy and even hurting someone else would remove you from society, to a place where you would give up all aspects of having to take responsibility for yourself. Is that what you really want? If it is, do not belittle the idea; open your mind to how damaging that might be to the way you are living your life to date.

- Have you ever wished yourself dead or thought about committing suicide?

At the end of each chapter you will find a section for your own personal diary entries but also in the last chapter, you will read some excerpts from other people's diaries. They are there for you to connect with and for you the reader to see the significance of keeping a diary. This diary is the first link to your inner child, your personal and intimate link to the part of you that is hidden behind a smiling face, or a jovial manner or various levels of intolerance towards others. I am encouraging you towards change yet I cannot give you the answer. I do not believe that any amount of diets, slimming clubs or self denial will make you change. Self love, self respect, and listening to the hurt part of you inside will take you on the first step of a thousand mile journey.

You have to start somewhere after all.

Your Personal Diary Entries

Do you use food to soothe your emotional distress?
Is food something you reward yourself with?
Write down anything that comes to mind from this chapter.
How do you see yourself in the future?
Do you want to live for a long time?

_____

_____

_____

_____

_____

_____

CHAPTER SEVEN

•

HOW DO WE CHANGE?

Throughout childhood and the pressures of our environment we can lose sight of ourselves because of the need to find love and attachment in security. The secret of our true identity lies within the realms of the child within. Reaching that lost child and reclaiming that innocence and spontaneity will, I believe, take you towards your true self.

Throughout our lives we learn to prove or show ourselves in a variety of ways; we experience life through what we see, touch, taste, hear and feel. We make sense of the world by making it material. Often unconsciously we build a frame of reference upon which to live life and, where there have been some cracks and or traumas in the process of development; we will have built a system of defenses to protect that inner child. Until we find that inner true self we merely live life as if on a stage, unreal, like a cardboard cut-out, living in a shop window, like a tailor's dummy, acting out life, aware of the world's eyes upon us.

How we sit, stand, and look will be on our mind.

We will be on guard, fearful of rejection by others or of offending someone, terrified of making mistakes, of being found out, shamed and caught out in mistakes or exposed in guilt, each of us tangled in the belief that the world *happens to us* and that we are not in control of our lives.

The word 'fate' holds such mysterious connotations and by using it we can hand responsibility for ourselves and our destiny over to this mysterious phenomenon, or, indeed to someone else.

Some of the solutions

According to research, weight that has been gained over a period of years simply cannot be lost in short periods of time with lasting effects. It describes carbohydrates as a frequent culprit contributing to weight problems, rather than simply too many calories. It sites patients as having what can be termed a carbohydrate addiction, a condition, probably genetically linked, in which the individual's body simply does not properly metabolise carbohydrates, mainly starches, snack foods and sweets.

As I stated earlier in the book this condition is linked with cravings, a longing for foods that contain carbohydrates. Even after eating a normally filling meal the compulsive eater will consider themselves hungry and will seek out more foods, which often contain sweet or starchy content. Finding themselves in a never ending circle of dieting and over eating, losing a little weight only to regain it again. Carbohydrate foods include potatoes, chips, bread, pasta, crisps, rice, chocolate, pastries, biscuits, sweets, dressings and so on. Even too much fruit could be a part of this process and yet it is the more healthy option.

It is my belief that this carbohydrate addiction cannot be cured, like an addiction the only way forward it to give them up. Of course there is no easy way to do this and as with alcohol the alcoholic cannot afford to drink again, as with the drug addict they must cleanse their system and then never touch drugs again. I can hear you already giving out the obvious comments, how can we give up food? Of course we cannot. So there in lies the problem. We cannot live without foods and we will struggle indefinitely with the carbohydrate cravings. **So what can be done?**

Personality Issues

I have proclaimed all the way through this book that knowing yourself first is the answer to a different way of life. What follows are some negative aspects to personality, which you will need to own and accept, because recognising your defences will lead you onto a path of self love and more choice about which path you want to take in life. As you go through the following section judge if any of the descriptions of behaviour relate to you on a scale of **1-10**. However all of us have some of the traits outlined to some degree, none of us are perfect and we will, under stress, often behave badly. I am asking you to think about how often and how much you do behave in the ways I have outlined. Once owned you have a choice to change.

1 Doesn't relate to you at all, **10** is definitely like you in a big way.

1—2—3—4—5—6—7—8—9—10

Suspicious Person

- Are you someone who looks inwards and who is suspicious of other people?

- Do you interpret other people's actions as deliberately demeaning, perhaps rushing into thinking that others think badly of you, seem threatening towards you in some way?

- Do you expect others to exploit you or expect them to treat you badly?

- Do you bear grudges and find it hard to forgive?

- Do you find it hard to confide in people?

- Are you quick to react with anger and do you reject others when you are upset?

- Do you find it hard to trust people?

Withdrawn and secretive

- Do you tend to act indifferently towards others?

- Do you maintain emotional distance from others?

- Do you have problems enjoying close relationships including being a part of a family?

- Do you prefer solitary activities?

- Do you experience strong emotions or not?

- Are you somewhat indifferent to praise and criticism?

Highly Emotional

- Do you feel that you need lots of attention, approval and praise?

- Are you overly concerned with your appearance?

- Do you express emotions without thinking about where you are or who you are with?

- Do you cry easily and soon feel hurt?

- Do you quickly express your anger without thinking about how to deal with problems?

Dependant

- Do you find it hard to make decisions without others opinions?

- Do you allow others to make your decisions?

- Do you find yourself agreeing with others even though you may think they are wrong?

- Do you do things that might feel demeaning in order to get close to others?

- Do you feel scared and uncomfortable when you are alone?

- Do you feel devastated about being left by anyone, or abandoned?

- Are you easily hurt by criticism or disapproval?

Perfectionism

- Are you preoccupied by detail, rules, lists, orders and schedules?

- Do you think that you spend too much time adhering to over detailing both in your social and professional life?

- Do you feel reluctant to allow others to do things because of the conviction that they will not do it correctly?

- Are you excessively devoted to work and productivity to the exclusion of leisure and friendships?

- Do you find it hard to make decisions for fear of making the wrong one, perhaps procrastinating or postponing?

- Are you overly conscientious, scrupulous and inflexible about matters of morality, ethics or values?

- Do you restrict your expressions of affection?

Secretly Rebellious

- Do you put things off that need to be done so that the deadlines are not met?

- Do you become sulky, irritable or argumentative when asked to do something you don't want to do?

- Do you work deliberately slowly or do you do a bad job on a task that you didn't really want to do?

- Do you often feel that others make unreasonable demands upon you?

- Do you sometimes avoid an obligation by claiming you forgot about it?

- Do you resent other useful suggestions concerning better productivity?

- Do you sometimes obstruct the efforts of others by failing to do your share of the work?

- Are you critical of those in authority?

- Do you sometimes flout rules and regulations?

You may not like any of the above questions but it is important to begin to recognise how you use your psychological and emotional energy in hiding the real you.

If you answer more than three questions in all from all or any of the categories past the half way mark, then most of the time you are defending the inner child, and

I urge you to think about how to change these aspects of your personality in order to start caring for yourself in a more positive way. You are using lots of emotional and psychological energy in a defensive position. You might want to talk to a therapist or counsellor about what you are discovering about yourself. Talking to a professional can be very helpful.

As a child matures its abilities emerge allowing it to grow into a self-sufficient adult. Healthy development occurs in a child who is self confident in self expression and results in an adult being able to face life's trails and challenges.

However, when a child faces abandonment threats, abuse and high levels of anxiety in its formative years there will be an injury to the sense of self. Thus as I have repeatedly stated throughout, the child will hide behind a false self, a self that protects the distressed child within. This is a defence originally developed to protect but which becomes an inhibitor to the 'real' connections in life. What was originally a safety mechanism becomes a self limiting process.

We all, as individuals, want to get basic needs met through the paths I described in Chapter Four (page 76) 'Hunger of a Different Kind'

A damaged sense of self will push us to find other methods of self satisfaction which are more likely to continue the damage such as self harming, eating disorders, drugs and alcohol abuse. This will be how we try to meet our own needs and block the way to satisfying the different and healthier pathways to a more fulfilling life and thus maintaining strong healthy patterns of behaviour in relation to self, other and the world around us.

> *In relationships an individual will cling or stay aloof and uninvolved emotionally out of fear of being hurt or rejected.*
>
> JAMES MASTERSON *(SEARCH FOR THE REAL SELF 1988)*

He recognised that intimacy is the capacity for two people to offer each other's real selves affection and acknowledgement in close ongoing interpersonal relationships. Therefore to manage and maintain a close, long term relationship with oneself and others we must be able to reveal and share what is deepest, truest or most real about our selves. If we are inhibited by powerful defence mechanisms how can we be true to either ourself or anyone else?

Hungers

As a child if our basic needs were met and if we meet them ourselves as adults in the here and now, we feel more solid as a person, more confident and more in contact with ourselves and others.

If however we now block those basic needs because as a child we had to find ways out of the distress, we are more likely to live our lives unhealthily.

> *'Those who strive to avoid contacting the core self often hold beliefs that they will be overwhelmed or engulfed by the intensity of such an experience. In an attempt*

to meet the hungers, but also to avoid connecting to their core selves they will develop unhealthy appetite paths.'

(J. MARDULA APPETITE PATH MODEL. TA.UK Nov 2001.)

According to Mardula's theory, when an individual has difficulty in *"being with"* themselves they will follow the urge to use, alcohol or drugs. They will not be able to take a healthy pathway of satisfying the unmet need inside. I believe that comfort eating comes into this category.

They see this as a way of avoiding what Mardula terms the *"unendurable"* distress inside. An overeater has forgotten, or never learned how to look for a healthy way to soothe the distress inside. To change this pattern one has to explore the different options.

Contact   Tell people how you feel, find someone you could telephone when you have the urge to eat when you don't need to. I suggest you join some kind of group, evening classes or learn some new sport or hobby where you will be able to increase the opportunity for meeting new people and making new friends. This is the way to nourish your sense of self worth. It is also important to make the effort in maintaining or rekindling old friendships.

Recognition   Begin to notice how people are towards you. Start listening to what they say and how they talk to you. Start to notice your own compassion towards others. Recognition is a two way-street, when you walk about with a smile then others smile back. I think it is important for you to recognise yourself and the roles you take in life. Are you someone's mum, grandma, teacher, friend and partner etc? Perhaps you are the life and soul of the party and people want you around, are you a loving wife or husband who acts in thoughtful ways? Maybe you do not realise the important place you occupy in the family, society or whatever, you need to see how important you are and how important others are to you, begin to change this and develop it. Consider if you are stuck in self-limiting places fulfilling other people's expectations which in time becomes a self-fulfilling prophecy. For those of you who gets lots of loving support and recognition for doing what you already do then consider carefully how you can yield more.

Incident   It is as important to plan incident into your life rather than just have it happen. Only you can make your life more interesting and more complete. Take up a new hobby, writing, learn a musical instrument, take singing lessons. Go for long country walks, learn something new like horse ridding or swimming, take up bird watching and make your life more interesting, only you can do that.

Stimulus   Listen to music, take up some kind of relaxation like meditation or yoga. Something creative that will fill the empty space inside and help you find the inner child which is the part of you that is creative. The importance with this one is that you really satisfy your senses. You might benefit from improving your working/living environment, by pampering yourself e.g. applying body lotion, getting some massage and or, by creating a space in your home where you can relax, take time to enjoy you garden if not, grow plants in plant pots and look after them carefully. Build this into your daily existence.

Structure   This is the need for security and to be in charge of one's life. Sometimes people have too much time structure and some not enough. Without a certain amount of structure we humans feel insecure and at worst meaningless. Even just planning a daily walk would satisfy several hungers at once. Keeping a diary and writing in it at a certain time of day every day is structured behaviour. Maybe keeping a pie chart, or journal on whatever things you do regularly that again shows opportunities for change or enhancement all of which might leap out at you. You will gain much in the way of satisfaction just by seeing how your day is structured in a positive way.

Remember!

Dealing with a food issue is a journey, it is a journey of self love, self discovery, this is no easy task and I cannot emphasis enough how keeping a diary of your journey, being completely honest with yourself in the diary and honest with others in your life will help. This will mean that you have to think about yourself all the time, indeed; whilst you are also thinking of others, you must repeatedly take into consideration what you want alongside being compassionate towards other people. You must take time to ask yourself the all important question

'What do I really want?'

None of this is about being selfish; it is about recognising your own importance. You are as important as everyone else, you matter and therefore you need to give yourself time to recover from a seriously painful condition. It will mean that you have to take care of yourself from scratch, possibly learning how to do this in ways you have never done before. Think of yourself as having just recovered from a serious illness and you need to have constant care from now on. Some days you will slip back into the old pattern but no matter, it's ok, go for it again.

Practice, practice, practice.

Remember that food has been a substitute for love, now I am asking you to give up thinking about food and think about **you**. Food is there, all around you and you can take it at any time; however, your love for yourself is not out there, it is inside of you and can only be found if you search deep inside. In the main all of you will be good nurturers, you will have looked after other people in more ways than one, not necessarily with food but perhaps putting them before yourself, saying yes when you mean no, doing things which you don't want to do, promising time to others thus reducing the amount of time you give to yourself. If you think about this you have spent a lot of time being untruthful.

Remember I do not have a magic answer or indeed a quick solution and that is not what this book has been all about, instead I am offering you the opportunity to seek the answer within yourself. Diet clubs and magazines will show how to get slim but not many show you how to stay that way. Diets prove you can lose weight very quickly in a short space of time, and diets do work but they require you to concentrate on the food itself. What are its constituents? Is it high in fat? High in carbohydrates? Low in calories etc?

They advise you to cut down on fatty foods, count calories, eat high fibre, increase your protein, but of course you will have done all that, been there, seen it, and done it! Someone like you will know how to diet but you won't know why you repeatedly have to, when others might not.

It is important you understand that this book has not been about how to diet, it is about how to recognise your own needs.

Needs that possibly have not been met for most or even all of your life? Saying no to others may be a part of the solution, but also saying no to you is just as important but saying no to yourself must be for the **right** reasons.

I suspect that those of you who have been yo-yo dieting and having a daily battle with your weight will be hoping for some magic cure, but sadly there isn't one. All of what you need to do will take time and patience, but I am offering some methodology. All of it is to do with time and the development of self love, patience and kindness to someone who is as important as you. You have seen the advert **'You're worth it'** try saying it until you believe it.

I do recommend Paul McKenna and his book and CD 'I Can Make You Thin' with the four golden rules he suggests. I believe his ideas are sound when you are ready, but it is **very important** to understand your own process first or you will not maintain the method he or any one else suggests without first learning what it was that hurt you so much in your history and acknowledge that although all that happened, it is time to take charge and responsibility for what goes wrong in your life today. You have a part to play now in not having looked after yourself, not loving yourself and not respecting you. You are merely continuing a negative pattern started somewhere in your history and you now need to take over and love the real self within.

Once you have explored the aspects of yourself that I am outlining in this book then it is time to concentrate on what you have been spending your life doing, not just eating badly or self harming but more to do with how you have been living with blinkers on. You have been living your life with tunnel vision. You have been seeing the world through a narrow perspective because most of your energy has been used to maintain a certain frame of reference. You have been suppressing painful emotions, and gearing all you do around that unconscious process.

Dare I say you have been living your life selfishly?

Yes! You saw right, selfishly.

You probably believe that you have been trying to live your life around others, trying to fit in, doing your best to get through life carrying a rucksack full of painful stuff, bemoaning the fact that you cannot change, and how out of control you feel. Think of all the lies you have told people, for example, when someone asks you how you are doing you tell them you are fine, or doing well, when in fact you are not.

Then there's the bit about doing things for others because you couldn't say no and then felt resentful about that. Now I ask you, 'Is that honest?' No of course not, but of course you never really thought about it like that did you? Answer the questions below and write down your answers in the diary section.

- Think about how you withhold from those you could be close to.

- How do you prevent yourself from being close?

- Do you resist close relationships?

- How might you fear closeness with another and what is your fear about?

- Do you fear being engulfed or swamped by others?

- Are you afraid that you might lose yourself in relationships with others not only sexual relationships but friendships and close intimate relationships?

- Are you afraid of being close because you are afraid of the loss?

- How many times do you do things for friends and family that you do not really want to do?

- How many times do you lie to people in your day to day life?

Just sit quietly for about 3 minutes and think about the following, I suggest you write down your observations. Don't forget the diary section at the end of each chapter.

- Are you or do you <u>observe</u> yourself interacting with others?

- Do you speak spontaneously or do you <u>censor</u> yourself?

- Do you give a <u>performance</u>?

- Are you <u>conscious</u> of how you sit, stand speak act express yourself emotionally?

- What is your worst <u>fear</u> in relationships?

- If you let go of <u>observing</u> yourselves what might occur?

- What is the <u>worst</u> thing that could happen if you make a mistake?

It is time now to let go of the following:

Let go of perfectionism
This means your expectations of yourself are too high. There is no such thing as perfection in the human.

Let go of pride, entitlement needs and control of your environment
Too much pride is about arrogance and perfectionism again. The world does not revolve around you. And you cannot take anything or anyone for granted. Trying to control the outcome to every situation only wears you out and alienates others.

Let go of your developed self image
You need to look at yourself through your own eyes, stop watching yourself through the eyes of others.

Let go of fear of criticism
You are your own worst critic and your fear is about what people will perceive about you and state openly. Once you forgive yourself for not being perfect, another's opinion will count for very little.

Let go of rejection issues

Rejection is about fearing abandonment as a child. Remember an adult cannot be abandoned; you are capable of surviving in the world as you are now grown up and have all your faculties and skills at your finger tips. As a child you feared abandonment because you needed others in order to survive.

Let go of fear of failure

What is the worst thing that can happen if you fail at something?

It is again to do with being abandoned as a child. If you fail to please the parent figures then you may have been rejected by those you needed and depended upon. The worst that can happen if you fail something as an adult is that you will give someone or yourself some problems. No big deal!

Once you let go you may find what lies beneath

You might have to feel shame, humiliation and vulner-abilities all of which you decided to protect yourself from as a child. You are a grown up now and you are not dependent upon anyone for your survival. You may feel sad or have to grieve the past but the way you live is not dependent upon others. You can survive your emotions. You now depend entirely upon you and you need to start making a better job of looking after you and the child inside who has been too afraid to mature.

Once you let go you will find a sense of who you really are? Find the child hidden for so long?

To do the following you will need to make space and time for you, with no interruptions or distractions.

Mirror

Look into a mirror taking at least 30 seconds to do this, build up over time. Look closely at yourself as if you are meeting you for the first time.

Forgo any feelings of silliness or embarrassment.

Do you like what you see?

Take time to do this exercise every day, as if you are getting to know a new friend.

Begin to have a conversation in your head with this person in front of you. You want to know about this person, what kind of things do they like to do?

What are their hobbies and interests?

How about their relationships with family, friends etc?

Ask about their childhood.

Then begin to accept that you are getting to know yourself.

In terms of childhood tell yourself what you know and what you can remember of significance.

What made you happy?

What made you sad?

Did you cry much?

How did you cope with the ups and downs of family life?

How have you been affected by your history, upbringing and general environment?

Remember!

Before we are free to love naturally we must deem ourselves loveable
When I say I love you I am saying?

You are important to me

You matter to me

I feel compassion for you

I feel empathy for you

I understand and accept you

I let you go freely'

We can only truly love others when we have learned how to love ourselves.

Try saying to yourself several times a day until you believe it.

I am important to me

I matter to me

I feel compassion for my self

I feel empathy towards myself

I understand and accept me

I am free to be me

If you can say these lines easily then well done, however, I doubt that to be the case right now. I suggest you consider why you don't feel important, or why you think you don't matter, you don't feel much compassion for you and so on?

Now ask yourself the following:

- Am I truly honest with myself and with others in my life?

- Why am I afraid to be honest with those I care about?

- Is it because I don't find myself loveable enough, so therefore if I am really myself they might reject me?

- Am I afraid they will not see me as lovable enough to have around?

I want to encourage you towards self love because it will improve all the following aspects of your personality

Self esteem,

Self respect,

Self confidence,

Self image

How can you love others honestly if you do not love yourself?

Loving yourself will give you the start to managing your food issue more easily.

Ask yourself the following questions

- **Who am I?**

- **What is my life all about?**

- **Why do I do the things I do?**

- **Is life the way I want it to be?**

- **Why do I behave towards me in the way that I do?**

- **Am I repeating old patterns?**

Finding the Child Within

You will need to read this exercise first then sit quietly to take yourself through it step by step. Remember you need time and a quiet space. Better still if you can find a true friend to read it to you and then share your experiences you will be fulfilling the first hunger of contact.

Imagine that you are going back to the house where you were a young child. You wander through the rooms remembering times you had, good and bad. Eventually you come to a bedroom where there is a full length mirror. You have never really liked looking at yourself in this type of mirror but this time you stop and take a moment.

You see yourself as you are today, an adult, looking back at you and although it is difficult for you to look. Eventually a child comes into view and you realise that this child is you as you once were at about three years old.

You begin to think about what life was like for you back then and the child stays in view looking back at the adult you.

How are you feeling?

What does s/he think of you now? Answer spontaneously from your heart.

Would s/he be happy with the way things have gone in your life?

Would they be happy with what you have made of yourself?

What do you want to say to this little you?

How do you feel as you see yourself as a small child?

Are you happy or sad right now?

Ask this child if they are ready to come back to you?

Ask yourself would they be safe enough with you?

Can you take care of them in a healthy way?

Do they want to be with you or have you abandoned them long ago?

If you take this child back into your heart it will mean that you have to think about them all of the time.

If this child wants to come back to you then they need to know that you will look after them better than you have been doing this far.

Are you ready to take on this responsibility?

What needs to change in you and your life to be able to do this?

More importantly ask the child if they want to be with you.

They may say no.

They may not think you are a good-enough parent.

You may have to promise to look after this part of you in a more healthy loving way.

It may mean you will need to take time learning new ways.

You might feel afraid of failing.

This child in you has long ago lost faith in being looked after in a loving way.

Try to keep the image of the child clear so you can now invite him or her into your heart and watch it merge with the adult you in the mirror.

When you are ready walk, away from the mirror leaving the house of your past forever, you should now have the child safely tucked inside you.

However if this child is reluctant to come back there may be a need to return here time and again until they do.

Without the child you are not fully conscious. This child is the real you.

To maintain a relationship with this inner you I suggest you find a picture of yourself as a child and keep it with you, looking at it several times a day.

Write down what you experienced in your personal diary section.

In conclusion I want you to go back through the book and look over the questions I have posed, you have probably just skimmed over them thus far, I suggest you write down the questions, taking time to think about your answers, then write your answers as best you can.

Up to now you have used food to block your true emotions and thoughts. It is time to seek out what matters to you.

Remember to write a diary. It is a way of expressing your inner most thoughts and feelings and you will find some release in this if you make a point in being disciplined about it, giving yourself the time. Your journal or diary is your friend and confidante it is the place to begin to find your true self. It will be hard at first but gradually over time it will become easier. There is no need to show what you have written to anyone if you don't want to.

Remember that if your self esteem is low you need to find out why. What needs to change in you for your view of yourself to change? I would urge you to find someone to talk to either a dear friend who will *not* put you down or try to justify why life is the way it is. Or go to a good therapist who can talk to you about body issues and self esteem, one who knows about comfort eating or self harming issues. Find a psychotherapist who will help you find the inner child and encourage you towards self love and self respect.

Throughout I have added some personal stories for your perusal and I hope they will give you some inspiration on this journey.

Remember that when someone believes they are worthless it is not because they are born that way. No one is born worthless, bad or useless etc. No baby comes into the world with a sense of low self esteem, each of us is born perfect and vulnerable and it is the environment we are born into which forms our opinion of ourselves and what we do with that. Of course I am aware that different cultures hold differing views of how ones world is formed but in most European countries of the world food and abundance are an issue for the modern individual particularly in Britain and America.

Remember to ask yourself the question
What do I really want?
Do I really want something to eat? Am I really hungry for food?
Or do I just want 'something' to satisfy the need inside?

Search your heart for the answer before you eat, look though the 'Hungers of a Different Kind' in order to know which or all needs satisfying.

Do I need any of the following hungers to be met?

Contact   Recognition

Incident   Stimulus

Structure

None of this is just going to happen to you, you have to make it happen because you are an adult. **You cannot relive childhood** and hope that someone is going to give you all the things you didn't get; you have to **go out there and get them yourself.**

Your Personal Diary Entries

Write down the results of your responses to the various things you have recognised about yourself in this chapter.

_____

_____

_____

_____

_____

_____

_____

_____

_____

CHAPTER EIGHT

•

DIARY EXCERPTS

Cheryl's diary

Day one Tuesday

I was scared of starting this liquid diet because I knew I would have to face my biggest problems of feeling so hungry.

It's evening now and my worst fears are being realised, the day started OK with the first drink and then I managed to last till lunch time feeling hungrier and hungrier then took the second meal in a drink which only eased the feeling a little bit. The afternoon has been awful, waves of nausea and even though I have drunk two litres of water throughout the day with still more to come, I have felt horrible.

The physical feelings have been the worst, the nausea and the dull headache starting in the back of neck and dull in side my head. I want to get into bed but am afraid that I might not sleep and then I will want to get up and have a snack in the night with a cup of tea.

I suspect that not only am I missing the amount of calories but also the tea and coffee I normally have with a small snack to tide me over from meal to meal. Carbohydrates!

I didn't think the morning would be bad but it's now the afternoon with the evenings being even more horrible, how will I get through?

Poor Stan is trying to be comforting, he made his own tea and hadn't eaten any snacks in front of me yet but I will go to bed soon and then he can have his bit of supper and a drink of beer as normal. My stomach is gnawing right now and I feel so sick and achy this must be withdrawal symptoms from the carbohydrates I suppose and also tea and coffee of course. It's a familiar feeling that is normally cleared by eating something or nibbling something. It's such a regular feeling that I never let get to this stage, never allow it to get out of hand and I feel scared of it. Not sure why!

I told Stan tonight that if every day is going to be like this then I know I will not be able to continue with this liquid diet for a week let alone a month. If I could get into the state of mind of being anorexic then I maybe could manage it but as yet there is only a low sense of resistance. Now I am in the position of wanting to drop the whole thing and go back to calorie counting but feel as if I am letting myself down as well as Stan and also everyone will think me weak. Even as I write that I know that is not true in the rational part of me. The only person my weight matters too is me.

Stan has just been in to the bedroom and was very good. He put his arms around me and I had a good cry, it all seems very silly, putting myself through this just to lose weight, I suppose if I trusted myself to count calories and stay below a 1000 I could do it just as well but maybe I cannot be trusted. I will see how I feel tomorrow and if it's too hard I will do two sachets a day and one light meal at night.

Wednesday

It's been better today, so glad I didn't have to go out or anything. I felt fragile this morning like I used to when I had migraines and vomited all day then the next day I felt cleansed somehow.

I am very much aware of my own battle with my self, with this need to try to feel better by eating but the problem is I do feel better for a while and without the food don't know what to do to make myself feel better. It is a dilemma indeed! The worst times of the day seem to be around three o clock in the afternoon, probably because we usually have a coffee and a biscuit which then tides me over to dinner in the evening. I can see that for most of my life I have kept hunger at bay by not allowing it to take hold, to do this I would munch or graze with nuts, bits of fruit all the things I perceive to be healthy but stuff that is pretty high in calories which just pile on the weight. Of course anything is unhealthy if you do it to excess.

All things in moderation they say, I wish!

I big part of me wants to drop all of this and go back to calorie counting but then I will have failed myself by not even completing a week. I could lose a lot of weight this week and then I will feel so much better and that is what I have to keep aiming for the end product.

Thursday

Last night Stan said it seemed to him like going cold turkey as in stopping smoking. Just stopping after 40 a day and that might be how I am feeling. Thank God I didn't ever learn to smoke as well, that would be hell. I do feel tired and my body feels painful. He said that when he gave up smoking he did it gradually but with this one has to do all or nothing and that is hard. The help line at slimming club said that the 3rd day can be the worst I hope to God not because yesterday is the worst I want to feel. I have been drinking a lot of water and that is pretty alien to me but I am doing it as prevention rather than having to do it as a cure when my head starts splitting

Today I have progressed onto weak Earl Grey tea with a saccharine in it which is reasonably tolerable. Gets better with each cup, I miss my milk and milky coffee in the morning but obviously I am suffering withdrawal from all Carbs like milk and cheese diary products in general.

Anyway once again Stan cooked his own tea sausage and mash, ohhhhh! Anyway I went into the bath after my soup and that felt OK, I should think by next week I will be able to prepare food for him and the grandchildren when they come over. Let's hope so, I feel a bit like an invalid but it will pass I am sure

Friday

I haven't had the chance to write in the journal but it hasn't been as bad only having liquids as it was the first few days. I managed to get buy at my daughter's yesterday but it hit me at the evening and I felt so hungry I had another one of the drinks that made four in the day, but I thought that better than having something 'forbidden'.

Today I have stuck with three of the drinks and didn't have anything until lunch time so that I could save one for the evening so I wouldn't go to bed hungry.

I have a strange state of mind and it's now become that I am afraid to eat normal foods.

I'll write more on this tomorrow

I did some meditation this morning haven't done any for a while but it did help. I meditated on feeling full and being slimmer. Throughout I did feel incredibly sad about what I believe I have to do in order to lose weight. I began to realise that my need to lose weight and then regain it over and over in my life must some-how be liked to the denial I experienced as a child. That's why I felt so sad.

Saturday

I have decided to go back onto a low carb diet, the med-itation each morning is helping and its bringing home to me that I need to look after myself differently than I have been doing.

Geoff

Diary entry

I think that food is my enemy. So maybe it's better not to eat at all. The way I get over this problem is to make a diet very strict so that I cannot detract from it. This is why I do various diets not giving much in the way of variety. Like the Atkins diet or a liquid diet, once on it I can stick to the rigidity of only being able to eat or take in certain foods and many others are forbidden. My problem is I don't really like anyone knowing that I am dieting because I would rather people think that I am just doing what's natural for me. I am not really excessively overweight for my height but that is because I am so rigid with myself. People think that I am quite naturally faddy about what I eat not that I am actually 'dieting' all the time.

I must say that eating out socially can be a problem when I am on a diet because there is so little on various menu's that I can eat, that makes me angry and irritable with the people I am with so sometimes it's best not to socialise. Most of the time life seems decidedly unfair, why do I have to put up with this constant battle with trying not to eat the 'wrong' foods?

I know that I will never be able to eat normally because I will gain weight, this all started as a kid when I got fat and got bullied at school when I got to about seventeen I decided that I had to diet and I have been doing it ever since. My wife just thinks that I am a faddy eater she diets as well but the difference is she doesn't realise that I am dieting.

I remember seeing an actress on the telly saying that she ate anything she wanted and never gained weight, then added quite calmly that she never ate more than two or three forks full of anything and always felt hungry. Another one was once asked how did she stay so slim and she said that she was always hungry and it had become a way of life.

I don't believe that anyone is naturally thin I believe that ninety percent of the population has to spend some time dieting in their life; I only wish I wasn't one of them.

Barbara's diary

Day 14

I am constantly wanting to row with Phil, my nerves are in shreds. I am not sleeping and feel frantic about my weight gain again. Started a diet two weeks ago and am now finding it terribly hard to keep up. I am not sleeping in fact last night I felt so angry with Phil I woke him up.

I think he's selfish and doesn't seem to want to help or support me. Why does no one understand what its like to be like this? Losing weight then regaining it, I truly believe that there is something wrong with me and I sometimes feel as if I am going mad.

I still have to do all the things that need to be done when I am on starvation rations. Cooking the children's meals, shopping for food and not being able to taste it for fear of a few calories, I feel so angry and hungry. My mother came over and that was another nail in the coffin, she cannot help herself and has to say things about my eating. I ate a dish of fruit salad with some grapes on top for lunch and she smarmily said 'aren't grapes fattening?' I felt like I was making some sort of metamorphosis from myself into a monster, like I could hit her over the head with a mallet. I was furious with her and sometimes hate the site of her. The old bag! We never got any fruit when we were kids and she has the nerve to come out with some supercilious remark as if she had been the best mother in the world.

Day 15

I am trying to stick with 1000 calories which does feel very harsh to some part of me. I feel very much as if I am denying something which of course I am, food, but deliberately withholding, which of course I am!

I feel such mixed feelings sometimes I just don't know what to do with myself.

Why do I put weight on so easily?

We did have a great holiday but then I came back with half a stone on and he comes back with no change. It makes me so angry because he drinks huge amounts of beer and eats one and two puddings after his dinner. Chips every lunch time, it's just not fair.

Kate's diary

Day ten

Got weighed on Tuesday which was the 8th day and lost 10lbs unbelievable!

It felt great and yet I wasn't happy. Very strange and perplexing but I told myself that what I am doing is marvellous. Billy is very impressed with what he calls my willpower but it's not really willpower its fear of losing what I have got. I know if I go back onto carbohydrates I will put the weight back on and this diet is very strict in its re introduction of carbohydrates. So I will stick with it now for a month. I know by next weighing day I will have lost over a stone in two weeks. By the end of the month I will have lost hopefully; two stone because I expect the loss to slow down after next weeks weight in.

In regards how I am feeling physically I suppose I can say I feel good but tired, sometimes exhausted, and I miss food terribly, especially the evening meal with Billy. Its part of our social time together, but I can feel the loss of weight all ready, I have been wearing a pair of trousers that wouldn't fit me for mucking about and they feel comfy which is amazing after only 10lbs. There is a strange unreality about it all as if I can't quite believe that I am doing something so radical.

Saturday 11th

Been an awfully difficult day today, I feel absolutely exhausted and just want to lie down. Billy is working hard in the bathroom to lay the new flooring. There has been a lot of rubbish from the old floor but I do not have the energy to help him at all. I feel guilty but at the same time just know I haven't the strength today. I am not sure why I should feel like this except that eating carbohydrates will give some energy and my body feeding on itself will not because it's a slower mechanism I suppose. I cannot say that I am hungry just feeling a bit lost really!

I have made his tea because he has been working right up to now and he said he would like quiche and chips I love quiche. However I left him to dish it up because he is watching football, I cannot cope with Manchester United and quiche and chips so have come upstairs to write in the diary whilst it's on. Normally each evening I have been having a nice bath but tonight cannot get into the bathroom. I feel irritable and angry but keeping it to myself.

I am hoping to get through a month on this diet but it's only a bit short of a fortnight and I am faltering. Maybe today is just a bad day. Perhaps I will feel better tomorrow?

I could do with some support right now but I know everyone will be having their teas as its only 6pm.

Feeling very sad and lonely right now.

Sunday 12th day

Feeling much better today mood has risen somewhat but not sure why.

Felt awful yesterday seem to have come through some turning point. It felt like a make or break day.

Lyn's diary

Diary entry

Being asked to keep a diary is a hard task for me. I am not that good at putting pen to paper or for keeping up routines, especially when it comes to doing something on a regular basis for me, it seems to fall by the wayside.

I am pushing 17 stone now and scared; I feel desperate and out of control as I don't seem able to get a handle on what to do. I know how to diet but just don't want to put myself through the torture of that whole system of cutting out the foods that make me feel good.

Maybe if I could stick to writing everything down then I might feel a bit better at least this way I know that there are other people out there like me.

My husband repeatedly tells me that my weight doesn't bother him and yet I am very much aware of how he eyes up slimmer woman and he is surrounded by woman at work. He insists he isn't interested but I just can't believe him. We haven't made love in a while and I am not sure if that is down to me or him.

I have gone onto a calorie counting diet today so will see how that goes. I know I don't feel in the right frame of mind but hey ho!

Finally put all of your diary notes together as a self help process towards making the changes you need. In six months or less, come back and look at how far you have come in learning to love yourself and take care of the little lost you inside.

Personal Diary Notes for future reference.

This is the place to write all the answers to the questions I have posed throughout the book and much more.

_____

_____

_____

_____

_____

_____

_____

_____

_____

_____

_____

_____

_____

_____

_____

_____

_____

_____

Acknowledgments

Eric Berne. *Transactional Analysis in Psychotherapy*. Souvenir Press, Condor Books. 1961

Eric Berne. *Sex in Human Loving*. Penguin Books. 1970

John Bowlby. *A Secure Base*. Routledge. 1988

John Bowlby. *Vol. 1. Attachment and Loss*. 2nd Edition London. Hagarth Press. 1969

John Bowlby. *The Making and Breaking of Affectional Bonds*. British Journal of Psychiatry, reprint. 1970

Richard Hycner. *Between Person and Person*. The Gestalt Journal Press, Inc. 1993

Nina Leick & Marianne Davidson-Nielson. *Healing Pain, Attachment, Loss and Grief Therapy*. Tavistock/Routledge London & Newyork. 1991

R.D. Laing. *The Divided Self*. Penguin Books Ltd. 1960

James E Masterson. *Search for the Real Self*. Free Press New York. 1988

J. Mardula. *Appetite Path Model*. TA.UK Nov 2001

Paul McKenna. *I Can Make You Thin*. Bantam Press. 2005

Ian Stewart & Vann Joines. *TA Today*. Lifespace Publishing. 1987

D.W. Winnicott. *Home is Where We Start From*. Penguin Books. 1986

William Worden. *Grief Counselling & Grief Therapy*. Tavistock Publications, London & New York. 1983

ISBN 142516181-2